# FOREVER CRAPS

# FOREVER CRAPS

## The Five-Step Advantage-Play Method

**FRANK SCOBLETE**

**Bonus Books, Inc.**
**Chicago, Illinois**

08  07  06  05  04          7  6  5  4  3

Library of Congress Control Number: 00-106979
ISBN: 1-56625-155-9

Bonus Books, Inc.
875 N. Michigan Ave., Ste, 1416
Chicago, Illinois 60611


Printed in the United States of America

*To the Captain's First Mate*
James Gallo, "Jimmy P."
*who now plays dice with God*

*Whose game was empires and whose stakes were thrones.*
*Whose table earth—whose dice were human bones.*

—Lord Byron, "The Age of Bronze"

# Contents

# Introduction

This is the craps book for players who are seriously motivated to win at this game and are disciplined enough to do it. It is going to be loaded with my personal experiences at the craps tables utilizing the techniques I discuss in this book and, more importantly, I am going to flesh out many of the ideas I have written about previously. In addition, I am going to give you a detailed biography of the Captain as thousands of readers have requested. This book is not an elementary book that explains how the game of craps is played. I have sections in both *Beat the Craps Out of the Casinos: How to Play Craps and Win!* and *Guerrilla Gambling: How to Beat the Casinos at Their Own Games!* (Bonus Books) that will explain the rules and procedures for craps. I am sure that if you are buying this book (or seriously considering buying this book) you want information that is new, relevant, and takes you where no craps book has gone before (with apologies to *Star Trek*).

Second paragraph reality check time:

"Mr. Scoblete, isn't craps a negative expectation game?"

"Yes it is."

"Mr. Scoblete, doesn't that mean that craps is unbeatable in the long run?"

"Yes that's what negative expectation means."

"Read your first sentence to this Introduction then. You're talking about a book that shows you how to *win at craps*, which is a negative expectation game, in the long run. So, correct me if I'm wrong, but it seems to me that you are saying that craps can't be beaten and can be beaten at the same time. Isn't that contradictory?"

"Yes."

"Would you care to explain yourself?"

"Yes. Craps is a negative expectation game that I believe can be beaten in the long run."

"That's ridiculous. How can such a thing be?"

"Read this book and find out."

And, dear reader, follow me, because after reading this book I hope your opinion of craps will be *forever* changed. Hence the title.

# ONE

# Many a No and Nary a Yes!

Craps. *Craps.* Let it roll "trippingly on the tongue"...crrraaaps! It's delightful, intimidating, thrilling, nerve-wracking, and the most enjoyable game in the casino. Craps. It has a veritable supermarket of bets to fit every taste, temperament and bankroll. Craps. Dozens of shouting, stammering, praying, groaning, cheering players hunched over a long table looking at a buffet of betting opportunities that can make the mouth water. Craps. Elemental, electric. Think about it, dream about it, but *whisper* it softly: *craps.*

Want a chance to win a lot of money with a little investment? Then try a one-roll bet of 12 that pays off at 30 to one. Want a chance to play a close game with the casino where the casino has almost no edge on you? Then try a Pass Line bet and back it with 10X odds. The casino will have approximately two Franklin D. Roosevelts worth of an edge for every Ben Franklin you bet this way.

Craps. Something for everyone. And that's good.

But that's bad as well. Because the more choices you have, the more of an opportunity you have to make the wrong choices and there are many more wrong choices to bet in craps than there are right choices . . . many, many more.

Yes, craps is exciting and, yes, played properly craps is one of the best games for the players to play in a casino. But craps can be the deadliest game. Lurking behind the facade of excitement and adrenaline rush are some of the very worst bets to be found in the casino; bets too many players make all too frequently. Bets that sink them and drown their bankrolls.

If you want a decent chance to win at craps tonight and tomorrow and in the long run (which I believe is possible utilizing the methods in this book) you must first understand that not all craps bets are created equal, nor are all craps *shooters*. We'll discuss the shooters in Chapter Five. As for the bets, some are decidedly inferior; belonging as they do to a classification of bets described by that legendary Atlantic City craps player, The Captain, as *Crazy Crapper* bets, because you have to be crazy to make them.

First a little background and refresher on the casino edge.

## How Casinos Make Money at Craps

The casino can make its money at craps in two ways. It can win more decisions against the player or it can charge a tax on the bets the player wins.

On the Pass Line and Come bets, the casino will win 251 decisions and the player will win 244 decisions for every 495 Pass or Come bets. That player shortfall of seven bets (251 - 244 = 7) equates to a casino edge of 1.414 percent on these bets (7 divided by 495 = .01414). Not bad at all. If you can afford to take the free odds bet, you can knock down the casino edge even more—to .18 percent in some casinos that have 10X odds (approximately two Franklin D. Roosevelts) and to .02 percent in those casinos that have 100X odds (two measly Lincolns per $100 wagered). [For my Canadian and European readers: .18 percent equals 18 cents per $100 wagered, while .02 percent equals two cents per $100 wagered.] Even double odds cuts the house edge to .61 percent. In short, these percentages make craps an attractive bet for the casino gambler despite the fact that the casino will win seven more times in 495 decisions. On a given night or few nights, craps is one close contest if played this way.

The second way the casino can win money from the player is not to win more decisions but to charge a tax on the player wins. Let us take the absolute worst bet on the craps table, the Any 7 bet. This is a one roll bet that the next number will be a 7. Since there are six ways to make the 7 out of 36 possible combinations, the probability of the 7 coming up on the next roll is six in 36 or one in six. (That means one winning bet in six decisions.) The odds are therefore five to one. You will lose five times for every one time that you win. Thus, if you bet five dollars on the Any 7, you can expect to lose a total of $25 on the five times that you lose.

What should you win the one time that you win? In a fair game, where neither you nor the casino had the edge, you would win $25 since the odds of hitting your 7 are five to one. However, the casino can't make any money on you if you get paid the true odds of the bet, so when you win, the casino comes in and takes 20 percent of your win as a tax, sometimes called "the vig" or "the vigorish." That's right. You only get $20 for a winning five-dollar bet on the Any 7 and not $25. The casino keeps that five dollars for itself. The casino has become your silent partner. When you lose you are a sole proprietor but when you win you have a partner! That 20 percent tax translates into a 16.67 percent edge for the casino on the Any 7. The Any 7 is sometimes called Big Red, the color your finances will be in if you keep making this bet.

This same sort of analysis can be made of all bets at craps. For example, the Field bet is a one roll bet that the 2, 3, 4, 9, 10, 11, or 12 will be the next number. At first this seems like an attractive proposition as there are 16 ways to make all those numbers. Added to that, the casinos will pay you two to one if the 2 or 12 hits, making it a "virtual" 18 winners (you win $18 on those 16 numbers). Wow!

Wow? No, POW!

The Field is a bad bet, though nowhere near as bad as the Any 7. Why? Because even with the two-to-one payoff on the 2 and 12 (and even money when the other numbers hit), the casino still has 20 ways to win and only 18 ways to lose (14 real losers and two double payments on two losers). That is a two-bet shortfall for the player which is the exact same edge that the casino has on roulette's even-money outside bets! What kind of edge does that translate into? If we count the 2 and 12 double payment as a "virtual" bet, the casino has a 5.26 percent edge (38 divided into 2 = 5.26 percent). Some gaming authors prefer to divide 36 real decisions into the two-bet shortfall coming up with a 5.55 percent edge for the casino. No matter. You get the picture. You aren't going to be coming home with very much money very often if you make the Field a steady betting staple.

Perhaps, the favorite bets of diehard Crazy Crappers (euphemistically called "action players" by the casinos) are the *Hardways*: the Hard 4, the Hard 6, the Hard 8 and the Hard 10. The Hardways are not one-roll bets. They are bets that the number(s) selected will be rolled as doubles (i.e., the Hard 4 is 2:2, the Hard 6 is 3:3; the Hard 8 is 4:4, the Hard 10 is 5:5) before either a 7 is rolled or an "easy" way is rolled. If you are betting the Hard 6, for example, you will win if it is rolled as a 3:3 and lose if the 7 is rolled or if a 6 composed of 5:1, 4:2, 1:5, or 2:4 is rolled. If you do win on a Hard 6 you are paid off at 9 to one. Great? Groan!

The true odds of the bet are actually 10 to one since there are 10 ways to lose (six ways on the 7 and four ways on the "easy" 6s) and only one way to win. If you were to bet five dollars on the Hard 6, you would lose $50 but only win $45 the one time in 10 that you won. Therefore, the casino takes a 10 percent tax when you win. This translates into a nine percent edge on the bet. All the Hardways can be so analyzed but why bother? They all stink. You make them and you are asking, no begging, for the casino to take your money. In short, the Hardways are a hard way to wrest money from the casinos.

And what about that bet of 12 that I mentioned in the second paragraph? Yes, the casino will pay you 30 to one if you hit that 12 on the next roll. But the true odds are 35 to one. If you bet five dollars on it, you win $150 every time you win but you lose $175 for every $150 you win. Yuch!

The following table shows the most paybacks and edges on various bets for the *Right* bettor. To refresh your memory, betting "Right" is betting with the shooter and against the 7. You're looking for the number to be made before that nasty 7 can show.

**The Wrong Bets for the Right Player**

| Bet | True Odds* | Casino Pays* | Casino Edge |
|---|---|---|---|
| Whirl | 20 to 5 | 16 to 5 | 16.00% |
| 2 | 35 to 1 | 30 to 1 | 13.89% |
| 12 | 35 to 1 | 30 to 1 | 13.89% |
| Hop (doubles) | 35 to 1 | 30 to 1 | 13.89% |

| Bet | True Odds* | Casino Pays* | Casino Edge |
|---|---|---|---|
| Horn | 20 to 4 | 17 to 4 | 12.50% |
| Hop (not doubles) | 17 to 1 | 15 to 1 | 11.11% |
| 3 | 17 to 1 | 15 to 1 | 11.11% |
| 11 | 17 to 1 | 15 to 1 | 11.11% |
| Any Craps | 8 to 1 | 7 to 1 | 11.11% |
| Hard 4 | 8 to 1 | 7 to 1 | 11.11% |
| Hard 10 | 8 to 1 | 7 to 1 | 11.11% |
| Any Craps | 8 to 1 | 7 to 1 | 11.11% |
| C&E | 15 to 3 | 13 to 3 | 11.11% |
| Hard 6 | 10 to 1 | 9 to 1 | 9.09% |
| Hard 8 | 10 to 1 | 9 to 1 | 9.09% |
| Big 6 | 6 to 5 | 1 to 1 | 9.09% |
| Big 8 | 6 to 5 | 1 to 1 | 9.09% |
| Place 4 | 10 to 5 | 9 to 5 | 6.67% |
| Place 10 | 10 to 5 | 9 to 5 | 6.67% |
| The Field | 20 to 18 | 1 to 1 (2 to 1 on 2/12) | 5.26% (or 5.56%) |
| Place 5 | 6 to 4 | 7 to 5 | 4.00% |
| Place 9 | 6 to 4 | 7 to 5 | 4.00% |
| Across the Board | 6 to 24 | (combination) | 3.90% |
| The Field | 20 to 19 | 1 to 1 (2 to 1 on 2, 3 to 1 on 12) | 2.63% (or 2.78%) |

*The right bettor is on the right hand side of the equation. For example, you bet one dollar on the Any Craps bet to win seven dollars.

## NEW WRINKLES ON OLD BETS

Right bettors are not just stuck with the above bets, of course. You can reduce the house edge significantly on Place bets by *buying* them. Traditionally, you pay a five percent commission as you "buy" the bet and then the casino pays the bet off at true odds. In the past, most Place bettors would buy the 4 or 10 for $20 by paying a commission of one dollar. That reduced the house edge to 4.76 percent, still awful, but not as awful as 6.67 percent on the Place bet. Then Las Vegas casinos allowed buying the 4 or 10 for $25, still paying that one-dollar commission. This reduced the house edge further. Now it was 3.85 percent. Then the Captain came along and bought the 4 or 10 for $35, still paying that one-dollar commission. The house now had an edge of 2.78 percent. What the Captain did was called "pushing the house" which is a technique whereby players attempt to get a better game than the casino advertises or is used to giving. The following is the list of current buy bets in relation to the original Place bets that could be available in your favorite casinos. These are not advertised, you make them and hope the casino will book them. Some are quite radical, for example, buying the 5 or 9 for $38. Very few casino dealers have seen that move but I have done it, as has the Captain, and the bet has been accepted. (By the way, the house edge of 2.56 percent makes this a bet to avoid. I made it to see if it could be done so that action players could reduce the horrendous four percent edge on placing of the five and nine.)

| Bet | Payoff | Commission | House Edge |
|------|--------|------------|------------|
| Place 4 or 10 | 9 to 5 | none | 6.67% |
| Buy 4 or 10 for $20 | 2 to 1 | $1 | 4.76% |
| Place 5 or 9 | 7 to 5 | none | 4.00% |
| Buy 4 or 10 for $25 | 2 to 1 | $1 | 3.85% |
| Buy 4 or 10 for $30 | 2 to 1 | $1 | 3.23% |
| Buy 4 or 10 for $35 | 2 to 1 | $1 | 2.78% |
| Buy 5 or 9 for $38 | 3 to 2 | $1 | 2.56% |
| Buy 4 or 10 for $39 | 2 to 1 | $1 | 2.50% |

In the rising competition for craps dollars some casinos have gone even further with the buying of the 4 or 10. You only pay the commission on the bets you win! Here's how the commission-after-a-win rule reduces still further the buy edges:

| BET | Upfront Commission | After Win Commission |
|------|--------------------|----------------------|
| Buy 4 or 10 for $20 | 4.76% | 1.59% |
| Buy 4 or 10 for $25 | 3.85% | 1.28% |
| Buy 4 or 10 for $30 | 3.23% | 1.08% |
| Buy 4 or 10 for $35 | 2.78% | 0.93% |
| Buy 4 or 10 for $39 | 2.50% | 0.83% |

While the above chart looks very impressive, and is, most casinos won't allow you to go over the $25 bet while still paying just that one-dollar commission when the commission is taken out on winning bets only. Still 1.28 percent is a not-too-terrible house edge to face if you are an action player and may even—in certain circumstances—be the preferred betting option as I shall show in Chapter Six.

## The Generous Casinos (?)

Some casinos, knowing that they need to attract more craps customers, have taken to lowering the house edge on many of the Crazy Crapper bets as well. For example, on the 2 or 12, some casinos might advertise that they pay out at 33 to one or on the 3 and 11 they'll pay out at 16 to one—a 5.55 percent house edge on all these bets. Certainly, 5.55 is a better percentage than 13.89 or 11.11. Still they aren't bargains. Nor is increasing the Hardways payouts on the 6 and 8 from nine to one up to 9.5 to one (a 4.54 percent edge), or increasing the Hard 4 and Hard 10 from seven to one up to 7.5 to one (a 5.55 percent edge). As I write this, there are even discussions that some casinos are going to offer the 2 and 12 at 34 to one which, would reduce the house edge to 2.77 percent. In light of the monumental house edges these bets usually entail, a 2.77 percent edge looks almost reasonable. Almost. Almost, that is, unless your intent in playing craps is to try to win money in the long run, then 2.77 is just too much of an edge to buck. The bottom line of Crazy Crapper bets is still this—you have to be crazy to make them.

## It's All in the Name, or How Casinos Psych Right Bettors into Playing Wrong

The best bets in the casino are usually bets with dull sounding names—the common-sounding Bank bet (1.17 percent house edge) or the drab Player bet (1.36 percent house edge) at baccarat, and, as stated, the Pass (1.414 percent house edge), Come (1.414 percent house edge) and Odds (no house edge) bets for right bettors at craps. Even in Sic Bo, a game known for its horrendous bets, the two best wagers are uninspiredly called the Big and the Small (both coming in with a 2.8 percent house edge).

Perhaps the single most exciting breakthrough in casino gambling in the 20th century for the average player was the development of Basic Strategy at blackjack. This allowed the player to play almost even with the house in single-deck games and with an approximately one-half percent house edge in multiple-deck games. And what did the player have to do to get such a good game? Just memorize a couple of dozen basic rules for the hitting, standing, splitting and doubling of hands. Still, the words "basic strategy" hold no allure; they are as bland as white bread. And the most exciting strategy discovery of all time for casino games, card counting at blackjack, sounds like something that can give you carpal tunnel syndrome of the mind!

Now, compare the above names for the above bets and strategies with the following and tell me which sound more interesting and exciting?

*Yo!, Yo-eleven!, Snake Eyes, Post Holes, Hardways, Horn, Horn-high-yo, World, Whirl, C&E, Hop, Boxcars, Big 6, Big 8, Big Red, Uptown, Downtown,* and *Across the Board.* Great names, bad bets.

*Yo!* is just another name for the one roll Crazy Crapper bet of 11. It has that hefty 11.11 percent house edge. *Yo-eleven!* comes by way of the Department of Redundancy Department since Yo is eleven. Same high edge—11.11 percent which is ironically appropriate for a bet called *Yo-eleven.*

How does *Snake Eyes* sound? Evil? It has an evil edge of 13.89 percent for the house because snake eyes just means you're betting that the two will be rolled next. The *Post Holes* are actually the *Hard 8,* and you know what poor bets all the hardways are already.

Want to bet the *Horn*? That's just a bet that the next number will be 2, 3, 11, or 12. You bet four units, one on each number. The house edge is in the double digits. The next one sounds intriguing, the *Horn-high-yo.* You bet five units, with two units on the 11. Double digits again on that house edge.

*Big Red* is our old enemy—the *Any 7.* The *World* and the *Whirl* are the same bets. You bet five units, one each on the 2, 3, 11, 12 and the 7. This is another double digit house-edge horror. *C&E* is a *Craps-Eleven* which is the same as the *Horn.* Want to bet on the *Hop*? Don't, because the house is extracting anywhere from 11.11 to 16.67 percent on any one-roll Hop bet. What is a Hop bet? It's either a dance or a one roll bet where you pick which dice faces will show.

The *Boxcars* bet is just the 12. The *Big 6* and *Big 8* are reserved for big dopes who bet even money that the 6 or 8 will appear before the seven. The edge is 9.09 percent. (If you just *place* the 6 or 8, you get a 7 to 6 payout and a low 1.52 percent house edge!) *Uptown* and *Downtown* are place bets that the 8-9-10 will show or the 4-5-6 will show respectively. *Across the Board*, merely means you are placing every point number (4, 5, 6, 8, 9, 10). Not a good move.

Why are the games, strategies and bets with the highest house edges the most alluring sounding? Since the substance of the games, strategies and bets leaves something to be desired, the name becomes the primary reason for playing the game, using the strategy, or making the bets. Frankly speaking, when Shakespeare asked: "What's in a name?"—the casino executives answered: "Everything!" And so it is.

Just watch the poor sods belly up to the craps table and feel like big shots when they say: "Give me a Yo-eleven, Boxcars, Snake Eyes and a five on the Hop!" and you'll know why the casinos love those fancy names. It is a way to psych right players into making the wrong bets and feel damn good about it to boot.

## Wrong Bets for the Wrong Bettor

The Wrong bettor (or "darksider") does not have any fanciful names to contend with, nor does the darksider have the wealth of betting opportunities that confronts the right bettor. Since so few craps players approach the game from this Wrong side, very little time has been spent developing fancy names for outrageous bets. In fact, there aren't many outrageous bets on the darkside of craps except for the Any 7. I have never seen a player on the darkside say: "Give me a no 12 for $37!" hoping to win a dollar. Maybe it's been done somewhere, sometime, but in all the thousands of hours I've spent playing the game, I have yet to see it.

| Don't Bet | True Odds* | Casino Pays | Casino Edge |
|---|---|---|---|
| Any 7 | 5 to 1 | 4 to 1 | 16.67% |
| Lay (buy) the 6 | 5 to 6 | 5 to 6** | 4.00% |

| Don't Bet | True Odds* | Casino Pays | Casino Edge |
|-----------|-----------|-------------|-------------|
| Lay (buy) the 6 | 5 to 6 | 5 to 6** | 4.00% |
| Lay (buy) the 5 | 2 to 3 | 2 to 3** | 3.23% |
| Lay (buy) the 5 | 2 to 3 | 2 to 3** | 3.23% |
| Place 4 to lose | 1 to 2 | 5 to 11 | 3.03% |
| Place 10 to lose | 1 to 2 | 5 to 11 | 3.03% |
| Place 5 to lose | 2 to 3 | 5 to 8 | 2.50% |
| Place 9 to lose | 2 to 3 | 5 to 8 | 2.50% |
| Lay (buy) the 4 | 1 to 2 | 1 to 2** | 2.44% |
| Lay (buy) the 10 | 1 to 2 | 1 to 2** | 2.44% |
| Place 6 to lose | 5 to 6 | 4 to 5 | 1.82% |
| Place 8 to lose | 5 to 6 | 4 to 5 | 1.82% |

* I've taken the liberty of expressing the odds in a rather peculiar way in order to keep them consistent with the fact that the player is on the right side of the equation. If we take a buy of the 6, the Don't player puts up six units to win five units, minus a five percent commission.

** Minus 5% commission.

# The Right Bets for the Right Bettor

Once we eliminate all the Crazy Crapper bets and some of the Place and Buy bets, the Right bettor is left with very few betting opportunities, all rather dull sounding. So what is a good craps bet? As a rule of thumb, I recommend that you try to keep the house edge to around 1.5 percent, preferably less. This can easily be done by betting the traditional Pass Line and Come bets with Odds or by placing the 6 or 8 in multiples of six dollars. It can also be done by buying the 4 or 10 when the house takes its commission only after a win.

| Bet | House Edge |
|-----|-----------|
| Pass/Come with 100X odds | 0.02% |
| Pass/Come with 20X odds | 0.10% |
| Pass/Come with 10X odds | 0.18% |
| Pass/Come with 9X odds | 0.20% |
| Pass/Come with 8X odds | 0.22% |
| Pass/Come with 7X odds | 0.25% |
| Pass/Come with 6X odds | 0.28% |

| Bet | House Edge |
|---|---|
| Pass/Come with 5X odds | 0.32% |
| Pass/Come with 4X odds | 0.39% |
| Pass/Come with 3X odds | 0.47% |
| Pass/Come with 2X odds | 0.61% |
| Pass/Come with 1X odds | 0.85% |
| Buy the 4 or 10 (commission on win only) | 1.28% ($25 multiples) |
| Pass/Come with no odds | 1.41% |
| Place the 6 or 8 | 1.52% |
| Buy the 4 or 10 (commission on win only) | 1.59% ($20 multiples) |

# The Right Bets for the Wrong Bettors

The darkside "Don't" bets are almost mirror images of the Right bets, albeit with fractionally lower house edges.

| Bet | House Edge |
|---|---|
| Don't Pass/Don't Come with 100X odds | 0.02% |
| Don't Pass/Don't Come with 20X odds | 0.10% |
| Don't Pass/Don't Come with 10X odds | 0.18% |
| Don't Pass/Don't Come with 9X odds | 0.20% |
| Don't Pass/Don't Come with 8X odds | 0.22% |
| Don't Pass/Don't Come with 7X odds | 0.24% |
| Don't Pass/Don't Come with 6X odds | 0.27% |
| Don't Pass/Don't Come with 5X odds | 0.32% |
| Don't Pass/Don't Come with 4X odds | 0.37% |
| Don't Pass/Don't Come with 3X odds | 0.46% |
| Don't Pass/Don't Come with 2X odds | 0.59% |
| Don't Pass/Don't Come with 1X odds | 0.83% |
| Don't Pass/Don't Come with no odds | 1.40% |
| Place 6 or 8 to lose | 1.82% |

There you have the no and the yes, the yin and yang, of craps bets.

Craps. A good game with many bad bets. Craps. For some astute players, a game that gives them a chance to wage a titanic struggle with the casino on almost even terms. Craps. For many, it is a bad game that ends up with their bankroll *being* the Titanic . . . sinking into the deep, dark ocean having hit a huge iceberg called the casino edge.

Craps . . . *Craps. Whisper it softly* . . .

# TWO

# The Theory of Advantage-Play Craps

With the exception of one or two strange bets here and there (buying player "don't" bets and the Captain's Oddsman's bet—see Chapters Nine and Eleven respectively), the theoretical underpinning of craps shows us quite clearly that the game is unbeatable in the long run. Period. Math is math after all and it doesn't make exceptions because we want it to. The math says craps is unbeatable. I can't, won't, and don't want to dispute that. How can I? One plus one equals two and nothing I can say, do, or desire can change that. Despite the fact that we can reduce the house edge to minuscule mathematical levels by employing the odds bets at 10X, 20X and 100X games, even the minuscule adds up to a mountain of money over sufficient time spans and that will spell a theoretical player defeat.

Even if we take the best possible scenario, a player who makes a one-dollar Pass Line bet and backs it with $100 in odds, the inevitable will happen if he plays long enough. He can expect to lose two cents for every $100 he bets this way. Of course, there will be huge swings of fortune, up and down, throughout his playing career but the math says that over sufficient time, he's going to be out two cents per $100 bet. Although the Odds bet is a fair bet, where neither the house nor the player has the edge, the Pass Line bet of one dollar has that 1.41 percent house edge grinding away at all times. And slowly, ever so slowly, amidst all the explosive ups and downs of a game played with $101 at risk during two-thirds of the Pass Line decisions, that smallish 1.41 percent on that measly one dollar will drain even a millionaire's bankroll to nothing—given enough time.

## Risk Time vs. Body Time

Time is one key to understanding the difference between the theoretical world of craps play and the real world of craps play. In the real world the player not only determines how much actual time he'll spend at the tables, but he determines how much risk-time he'll spend as well. In fact, the player determines where, when and on whom he'll bet.

Risk-time is a very simple concept. It boils down to how much of your body time at the table is actually time when your money is at risk. In roulette, for example, your money is at risk on every spin. You either win or you lose. If your body is there for one hour, you are at risk for one hour if you bet on every spin. Of course, roulette is a rather slow game so that one hour might not consist of all that many decisions. Contrast that with mini-baccarat where your money is at risk approximately 90 percent of the time (as long as you aren't risking money on the Tie bet, that is) but you're still getting 120–160 decisions in that 90 percent of an hour's play. That's a lot of risk!

At craps, your money is not really at risk on every roll because often no decision occurs on a given roll—sometimes your money doesn't get acted upon many rolls in succession. For example, if you bet the 6, the next roll of the dice contains only 11 possible decisions for you (five 6s and six 7s) while there are 25 possible non-decisions. When mathematicians talk of the long run, they usually mean millions of *decisions*, not millions of actual rolls. When you read the figures for the Pass Line bet (251 losses, 244 wins) you might have thought of that as 495 consecutive rolls of the dice. It wasn't—it isn't. When the shooter is on the Come Out roll, there are only 12 decisions possible on the Pass Line—the winning 7 and 11, and the losing 2, 3, and 12. The other 24 numbers are "no decisions" because you neither win nor lose your Pass Line bet. If we assume that a dice game at a moderately active table has approximately 70 rolls per hour, it would take a very long time for 495 Pass Line decisions to occur. It might take a thousand or more rolls!

Of course, most players don't simply bet one number. When I finally have my money at risk I prefer being up on three numbers. If we take the three numbers with the highest hit frequencies 6, 8, 9 (or 5), we can see that our money will be theoretically "acted upon" an average of 20 out of 36 rolls (five ways to make 6, five ways to make 8, four ways to make 9 and six ways to make the dreaded 7).

Why is it important to understand the idea of risk-time? Because your per-hour loss expectation is markedly reduced by the fact that you aren't really involved in every decision. And why is that important? Because the casino raters who determine your comps aren't really analyzing the body-time to risk-time ratio. They rate your play based on body-time and therein lies one opening for getting more back in comps than you are giving away based on your mathematical expectation.

How important are comps in the formulation of an advantage-play theory of craps? They are very important for some players . . . and not important at all for other players. Comps are merely icing on the cake for rhythmic rollers who might—through their shooting—actually be turning the tables on the casinos by getting a *mathematical* edge. But comps can be a *major source* of income for players looking to get a *monetary* edge over the temples of chance. There is a difference between a mathematical edge and a monetary edge, although a mathematical edge usually yields a monetary edge if the player manages his bankroll properly. The mathematical edge is real, concrete and will determine the long-run prospects of a player. Play "W" number of hours with "X" percentage of an edge and you can expect to win between "Y" and "Z" amounts of money. That's a hard, fast rule.

If I have, for example, a one percent edge in a coin flip, I'll win 101 decisions and lose 99 decisions on average. In the short run, that one percent edge doesn't look all that powerful as I could lose many flips in a row and need a hefty streak to catch up. But over hundreds of thousands, and millions of flips, sooner or later, I am going to catch up and start winning some money—as long as I have the bankroll to sustain vicious losing streaks. And the longer I flip, the more I'm going to win. Naturally, a huge chunk of time will be needed to assure a win, and an ample bankroll, but given the edge, given that chunk of time, given that bankroll, the win is mine guaranteed. (That's the world of theory. In the real world, I could start flipping that coin, lose for several days, get hit by a bus, and end up a loser on my way to the pearly gates.)

That's why the casinos can bank on winning from the players. They have the time (all those tables going 24 hours a day), the bankroll to capitalize their venture, and the edge. With so much action, spread out among so many players, the casinos hit the long run in short order. It is rare that craps loses money for any given casino on any given month because even if several tables have several days of blistering rolls by many shooters, they will have many more days of rotten rolls by many more shooters on many more tables.

## The Monetary Edge

The *monetary edge* (as I've coined it) is a more subtle concept and is not the same as a mathematical edge. It means that through comps (free or discounted rooms, free or discounted meals, shows, what-have-you), the monetary value returned to the player is slightly greater than the expected loss by the player in order to get that value. Simply, if I played four hours, and expected to lose $12 by my playing methods, but get back $40 in comps because of my style of play— I'm $28 ahead of the game. But I am not ahead at the *craps* game, rather I am ahead of the *money game* I'm waging against the casino. I want to get more from them than I am giving them. Indeed, to formulate the "ultimate attack on the casinos" it is necessary to understand and put into practice the five basic principles of advantage-play craps.

## The Five Steps of Advantage-Play Craps

**Step #1:** *Play the 5-Count and don't risk money on every shooter.* Bet on every shooter and you will lose. Even if there are some shooters out there in casinoland who can actually control the dice (and I now firmly believe there are), they are few and probably far between. The legion of craps shooters are long term losers *and* short term losers as well. You must have a method for selecting those shooters that you will bet on and those shooters you will avoid. Shooter selection will comprise a two-part criteria. Part one is the utilization of the Captain's *5-Count*, a method for shooter selection that I have written extensively about for over a decade now.

**Step #2:** *Develop a rhythmic roll.* You can't force other players to take care with their shooting styles, but you certainly can take care with your own. Developing a rhythmic roll is essential for advantage-play craps. A rhythmic roll is one where you attempt to control the numbers that come up when you shoot.

**Step #3:** *Utilize the Golden Ruler.* Once shooters have made it past the *5-Count*, a secondary criteria must be used for determining whether to risk money on them. This is the Golden Ruler principle that shows us which *5-Count* shooters to bet on.

**Step #4:** *Utilize the best betting methods for your purposes.* If you are playing to get comps, you might want to give the casino a slightly higher edge in order to get greater value in your comps. If you are looking to capitalize on a known rhythmic roller's numbers, then you might decide to bet traditionally or to employ the Captain's Supersystem.

**Step #5:** *Give less action but get more comps.* If you are making an attempt to get comps as a means of gaining a monetary advantage or to enhance your actual edge, the idea is to get more value than your action warrants.

There's the outline of what it takes to gain a real-world advantage over a theoretically unbeatable game. Now, let's explore the ins and outs, the nooks and crannies, of just how it's done. In the coming chapters I will deal with each of the five principles and show you how to employ them to get an advantage at a negative expectation game.

# THREE

# Step # 1: The 5-Count

*"The 5-Count is the most intelligent method I have ever seen to reduce your exposure to rotten shooters and position yourself to take advantage of possibly good shooters. Since playing it, I have been winning consistently. Thank you, Captain!" —Craps Player A*

*"The 5-Count is the stupidest thing I ever heard of. What do you do, sit around with your hand up your butt waiting for five rolls? What kind of fun is that? I go to the casinos to have fun, not to hang out waiting for some stupid magic formula to kick in. I wouldn't play it if you paid me." —Craps Player B*

*"Hey, it can't hurt to play it, right? It doesn't increase your chances to lose, does it? It has no down side. So why not play it?" —Craps Player C*

Since the publication of *Beat the Craps Out of the Casinos: How to Play Craps and Win!* more has been written, both pro and con, about the *5-Count* than about any other aspect of the Captain's methods of play. Not a day goes by on the Internet message boards of gambling sites when someone doesn't praise it or damn it or analyze it or wonder about it. That makes sense, of course, since the *5-Count* is at the root of all the Captain's methods of play.

Three basic camps have developed over the years. Camp One is represented by "Craps Player A" of the first quote above. These are people who have employed the *5-Count* over prolonged periods of time and found what I have found—it works. It works not only to reduce your exposure to the house edge, but to give you a slight overall positive expectation at the game. Camp Two is represented by the "Craps Player B" of the second quote. These are players who have not played the *5-Count*, or played it a few times, but hate the very thought of it. Some of these players are well-schooled in the math of craps and in the fundamentals of sound casino play which, translated, means they don't believe there is a chance in heaven to overcome the negative expectation of the game. Camp Three is represented by the "Craps Player C" in the quotes above. These are individuals who are the craps equivalent of agnostics. They aren't sure that the *5-Count* works to actually win money, but they sure understand that it works to reduce their exposure to the house edge by limiting the number of shooters they risk their money on.

In the 10 years since the *5-Count* exploded on the craps players' consciousness, 10 big questions have arisen concerning it. Here they are with the answers.

# The 10 Big Questions on the *5-Count*

## 1. WHAT IS THE PURPOSE OF THE 5-COUNT?

If you bet on every shooter in craps, you're dead. No matter how many rhythmic rollers are out there; no matter how large your bankroll, sooner or later, the incredible barrage of "random rollers" will kill you. As the Captain says, the dice can be shot out of a small cannon and there would be good rolls just because that's how randomness works. There would also be mediocre and rotten rolls . . . many, many rotten rolls. And when all was said and done—the casino would win its percentage based on your betting patterns and you would lose because in a random game, the math of craps wins out over our desires.

The *5-Count* is the Captain's method for deciding which shoot-ers to bet on in the real world of casino play. It has a simple and clear purpose—to offset the math. It does so in the following five ways:

1. By locating shooters who are conscious rhythmic rollers. These shooters are consistently turning the odds to slightly favor the players.

2. By locating temporary rhythmic rollers who on any given night are turning the odds to favor the player.

3. By allowing our money to last over longer periods of table-time so that should a hot shooter come along—be that shooter a ran-dom one, which is most likely, or a rhythmic one, which is less like-ly—we have not lost so much money that we can't come all the way back.

4. By helping us to avoid the horrendous shooters who seven out early. These are the shooters that you generally don't make any money on, the very shooters that usually put you into a deep hole that even epic rolls can't get you out of.

5. By allowing us to get more in comps than we actually merit. The *5-Count* can give a player a four-hour rating when his money was at risk for only two hours. It is quite possible, therefore, to get comps that literally give us a monetary edge over the casino.

## 2. WHAT PERCENTAGE OF THE SHOOTERS DOES THE 5-COUNT ELIMINATE?

Based on my experience, approximately 50 percent of the shoot-ers on a given night will be eliminated by the *5-Count*. The over-whelming majority of these shooters seven out in such a way as to cost the players who bet on them dearly. For example, the shooter establishes his point and the "action players" start placing the 6 and the 8, and buying the 4 and 10. The shooter rolls a garbage number, then sevens out. The "action players" have been creamed, losing two, three or four bets on one horrendous roll. Craps is a very tough game because of one fact: When you win, you win one bet at a time, but when you lose to that 7, you lose all your bets at once. So the over-whelming majority of the shooters who seven out before the *5-Count* is completed will be losers for the other players.

## 3. ARE ALL SHOOTERS WHO SEVEN OUT BEFORE THE 5-COUNT AUTOMATIC LOSERS FOR THE PLAYERS?

Not all pre–5-*Count* shooters are losers. Some shooters will establish a point number, come right back and hit it; establish another point and then hit that; then establish another point and bam! seven-out! Those of you reading this who already play the 5-*Count* have probably seen this sequence in some way, shape or form: A shooter hits several numbers in a row before sevening out just after the 5-*Count* and just after you've placed your money at risk. Indeed, the worst evenings for 5-*Count* players are just such evenings when many shooters make it to the 5-*Count* only to seven out soon after. *If craps were strictly its mathematical underpinnings, as many shooters would seven out early after the* 5-Count *as would seven out early before the* 5-Count *because the math does not distinguish one roll from another.* But in the real world of rhythmic rolling, dice controlling, casino-comping play, the 5-*Count* allows us to save money, stretch our time at the tables without the attendant risk, and give us the best possible chance to be there when (or if) those good rolls occur.

## 4. WHAT IS THE ACTUAL 5-COUNT?

The shooter is on the Come Out roll—as soon as he establishes a point that is the 1-count.

The second roll, no matter what the number—except for a 7 which means he sevened out—is the 2-Count.

The third roll, no matter what the number, is the 3-Count.

The fourth roll, no matter what the number, is the 4-Count.

However, the fifth roll must be one of the *point* numbers—4, 5, 6, 8, 9, 10 to achieve the 5-*Count*. If the fifth roll is a 2, 3, 11, or 12, you are at the 4-Count and holding. When he rolls the next point number you are at the 5-*Count*. Now, you will place money at risk.

If a shooter sevens out—you begin all over again with the next shooter.

Okay, let's do a few scenarios to get a feel for the 5-*Count*:

A new shooter is passed the dice.

He rolls a 7. No count because the 7 is not a point number.

He rolls an 11. No count.

He rolls a 4. That is a point number and it is also his point. 1-Count.

He rolls a 4. He has made his point. 2-Count.

He rolls a 7. This is the 3-Count. (Remember he is on a new Come Out roll and the 7 is now just another number for this particular shooter at this particular point.)

He rolls an 11. This is the 4-Count.

He rolls a 3. This is the 4-Count and *holding*.

He rolls a 6. This is the *5-Count*. It also becomes the shooter's new point. You will now risk money.

## 5. IF THE SHOOTER MAKES HIS POINT DO WE START THE 5-COUNT OVER AGAIN?

No. Even if he should roll some 7s as a part of his Come Outs, once the same shooter has successfully made the *5-Count* we stick with that shooter. So if a shooter makes his point and then on a new Come Out he rolls a string of 7s—that's fine.

The *5-Count* is to help us avoid bad rolls and position us to take advantage of good ones. It's a cut and position kind of method—cut down exposure to the house edge and position us to be at the table for the good shooters.

## 6. HOW DO YOU PLACE MONEY AT RISK WHEN YOU USE THE 5-COUNT?

There are any number of ways to place money at risk using the *5-Count*. However, there are three major ways to do so:

1. Place betting.

2. Traditional Pass/Line and Come betting with odds.

3. The Captain's Supersystem

There are also any number of ways to "time" when your money goes on the board. Many of these I have covered in my two previous books *Beat the Craps Out of the Casinos: How to Play Craps and Win!* and *Guerrilla Gambling: How to Beat the Casinos at Their Own Games!*

## 1. *5-Count* Place Betting

Place bettors simply go up after the *5-Count* is completed by placing the 6 and 8 in multiples of six dollars. If the casino where you play allows buying the numbers with an "after-win commission" as opposed to a traditional "up-front commission," then you can also buy the 4 and 10 for $20 or $25 (if you can afford it). You have to decide how many numbers you want to be on—you might just want to place one or two numbers if you are on a limited bankroll. Or, if you are the aggressive type and don't mind the risks inherent in betting four numbers, you might want to go up on the 4, 6, 8, 10. I tend to go up on three numbers at first.

## 2. *5-Count* Pass and Come Betting

Pass Line and Come players first have to decide how many numbers you want working before you can decide at which point to place money at risk. Let us say that you want to be up on three numbers when the *5-Count* is completed. Here's how you could accomplish that:

Shooter rolls a 4 = 1-Count.

Shooter rolls a 6 = 2-Count.

Shooter rolls a 2 = 3-Count. Now place a Come bet.

Shooter rolls a 9 = 4-Count. Your Come bet goes up on the 9. You now place another Come bet.

Shooter rolls a 6 = *5-Count*. Your second Come bet goes up on the 6. You now place odds on both the 6 and the 9. You also place another Come bet.

Shooter rolls an 8 = 6-Count. You put odds on the 8. You are now up on three numbers.

In a scenario such as this, any time one of your numbers hits, you immediately put a Come bet up to bring your total to three numbers working. If you wanted to go to four numbers working, you would keep putting up Come bets until you were up on four numbers.

However, not all Pass and Come scenarios are as simple. What if the shooter makes his point just as the *5-Count* is reached. Do you have your bets working or not working? The Captain says to let the normal course of the game predominate, which would mean *not* having your numbers working. Let's take a look at how this would work:

Shooter rolls a 9 = 1-Count.

Shooter rolls a 6 = 2-Count.

Shooter rolls a 6 = 3-Count. Place a Come bet.

Shooter rolls an 8 = 4-Count. Place a Come bet.

Shooter rolls a 9 = *5-Count*. Shooter has made his point. Take odds on your 8 and 9. Place a Pass Line bet. Keep your 8 and 9 odds *not-working* which would be a normal procedure for most casinos. When the shooter establishes his next point, take odds on the point and your three bets are now working. The Captain believes that the added comp benefits of having the bets not working on Come Outs—but still counting towards comps—is another reason to stay off during Come Out rolls. In addition, certain rhythmic rollers have different dice sets for their Come Out rolls where they wish to increase the appearance of the 7, not decrease it. If your odds bets are working on these Come Outs, you're asking for trouble.

## Combining Pass, Come and Place Bets

Some players like to combine Place bets with traditional Pass betting. When the *5-Count* is completed, they go up on the 6 and 8 and then place a Pass or Come bet in order to get up on the other numbers (or replace the Place bets). Place bettors, of course, get much better ratings in the casino comp game than do Pass and Come bettors because many casinos *do not count* the odds bets when they figure average bet-per-roll statistics. So someone who places $30 on the 6 and $30 on the 8 is rated as a $60 player, while someone who has a $10 Come on each of these numbers and puts $25 in odds on each (the same $60 at risk) is only rated as a $20 player—the amount of the combined Come bets. In some scenarios, for comping purposes, wise *5-Count* players will utilize Place betting to win the money game with the casino in order to get a monetary edge as I'll show in Chapter Seven. Place betting can also be the method of choice for certain rhythmic rollers as I shall show in Chapter Six. Unfortunately, most Place bettors get hammered by the large house edges on the 5 and 9, 4 and 10 in order to get into the action fast. However, by placing the 6 and 8, such bettors can get good comps points but only face a maximum 1.52 percent house edge. This also holds true for buying the 4 and/or 10 in casinos that allow the paying of commissions on wins only.

### 3. The Supersystem

The most controversial method utilizing the *5-Count* is the Captain's *Supersystem*. Here the player is using the "Doey-Don't" style of betting in order to play the odds. A player simultaneously places bets on the Pass/Don't Pass and/or on the Come/Don't Come and when the wagers go up on the numbers, the player takes maximum odds. At first look this seems to be a foolproof system as the Do (Pass and Come) and the Don't (Don't Pass and Don't Come) cancel each other out. When the 7 and 11 are rolled during the Come Out, the Do bet wins, the Don't bet loses. When a 2 or 3 is rolled, the Do bet loses but the Don't bet wins, however. The problem with this type of wagering is the fact that the 12 is not a washout but rather costs the Pass Line bettor his bet while pushing on the Don't side. How often will Boxcars be on track for a Come Out roll? One in 36. So if you are betting on the Doey-Don't, on average you'll get up on the numbers 35 times without the casino having any edge on your bets, but on the 36th roll (which can, obviously, occur at any time) you will lose the Pass Line portion of your bet. Whack!

This style of betting is somewhat less mathematically attractive than straight Pass/Come betting because in those 36 rolls, the player faces a house edge of 2.78 percent which is slightly less than double the Pass/Come house edge of 1.414. Recall that in 495 Pass Line decisions, the player has a seven bet shortfall (251 to 244). In 495 Doey-Don't decisions, the player will have hit that 12 approximately 14 times. So why would the Captain, the greatest craps theorist of all time, advocate this system of betting if it is mathematically somewhat inferior to regular Pass Line and Come betting? Also, why would some casinos from coast to coast—in Atlantic City, Nevada, and Tunica—ban the Captain's *Supersystem* which is merely utilizing the *5-Count* with the Doey-Don't style of betting?

The answer has to do with the nature of the game as it is played in the real world of the casinos—a world where casino executives are fully aware of the fact that some people control the dice and can change the odds of the game to favor the player. One casino executive told me: "I'm not stupid. I've been around a long time and I know what some players are capable of. Dice control is not a fiction, it is a fact. And I watch for it."

So why use the Doey-Don't?

When a shooter passes the *5-Count* and begins a torrid roll, the 7 is the one number that rarely comes up or comes up not at all. Remember that it is the one in six appearance of the 7 on the Come Out, after all, that helps give the Pass Line player his two-to-one "edge" (actually the 7 is three-fourths of the reason for the edge) during this portion of the game. Once the number is established the odds turn wildly in the casino's favor. Reduce the 7's power on the Come Out roll and you reduce the Pass Line wager's importance in reducing the house edge. In fact, during hot rolls, where the 7 has all but disappeared from view, you are giving the casino a nice chunk of your Pass and Come wagers *every time you win* your bet at even money. Not so with the Odds bets. These are paid at true odds and during a hot roll, the money on them comes rolling in without the casino as your partner. Indeed, if the *5-Count* is helping to locate rhythmic rollers, such as Sharpshooter and his buddies, whose 7 to number ratio is one in seven, one in eight, or one in nine, etc., it is quite possible that the Doey-Don't might be the preferred method of betting. Certainly in hot rolls, you don't want to share your money with the casino.

But wouldn't the reduction of the 7 merely increase the appearance of the other numbers proportionally, thus increasing the appearance of the 12 as well? Perhaps. Even if it did marginally increase the appearance of the 12, that fact would be more than offset by constantly getting even money on your Pass Line and Come wagers during hot rolls. That's the trade-off. You are looking for real-world rolls by playing the *Supersystem*, not just theoretical ones, or computer-simulated ones, based on randomness. You're looking for shooters who are controlling the dice, consciously or unconsciously, and the Doey-Don't puts the maximum money in their line of fire—on the Odds bet portion of the game, not on the Come Out portion.

The second reason for the Captain's advocacy of the *Supersystem* is somewhat more mundane. It reduces the overall fluctuation of your bankroll because you are essentially betting less money. Granted, the house has a slightly greater edge on the money you do bet, but that's an exchange bettors on short bankrolls might be willing to make and that a few good post *5-Count* shooters will more than make up for. And keep this is mind, when the full odds go up on the numbers using the Doey-Don't style of betting, the mathematical difference in the house edge between that and the traditional Pass Line and Come wagers is in the tenths of a percent.

So how do you get up on the numbers using the *Supersystem*? Let us say you want to be up on three numbers when the *5-Count* is completed. Here's one way you could do it:

Shooter rolls 10 = 1-Count.

Shooter rolls 8 = 2-Count. Place a Come/Don't Come bet.

Shooter rolls 6 = 3-Count. Place a Come/Don't Come bet.

Shooter rolls 9 = 4-Count. Place a Come/Don't Come bet.

Shooter rolls 5 = *5-Count*. Take Odds on Come numbers (8, 9, 5).

## 7. WHY DOES THE 5-COUNT HAVE TO START AND END WITH POINT NUMBERS? WHY NOT JUST ANY FIVE ROLLS?

There is a definite method in the Captain's . . . methods. Certainly, hot shooters who have long epic rolls win us money because they are hitting a multitude of numbers, some of which will be ours. But the definition of a good shooter transcends that of an epic roll. Shooters who have relatively short rolls where they hit a repeating number or several repeating numbers can also make us money. These are "good" shooters, too. "Any shooter that makes you money is a good shooter," states the Captain.

Indeed, many rhythmic rollers are specialists in certain numbers. Read Larry Green's comments about his 6s and 8s in Chapter Four. One rhythmic roller, who preferred anonymity, said: "For me, it's the Hard 4, that's my number. I make it much more than once every 36 rolls. My game is to buy the 4 and put a bet on the Hard 4. This is when I am rolling. So I'll have a Pass Line and a 4 and a Hard 4. That's my money number. I don't usually have big rolls but I almost always hit that 4—and often it's the Hard 4—before I seven out."

The reason the *5-Count* begins with a point number and ends with a point number is an attempt to ferret out the shooters who will repeat the point numbers (4, 5, 6, 8, 9, 10)—in rapid succession—and make us some money. We don't want the 2, 3, 11, or 12 repeating because we don't want to get into the habit of betting these numbers.

The house edges are just too great to overcome. Thus, when the 4-Count is finished, we want that fifth number to be a point number in the hopes that the shooter will get into a repeating number rhythm. If it isn't a point number, we go into a hold pattern.

"How often have you seen this at a craps table," asks the Captain. "A shooter is on the Come Out and he rolls two or three 7s in a row, establishes a point, rolls one or two garbage numbers, then sevens out just after five rolls. If you started the *5-Count* with any five completed numbers, a shooter in a repeating 7 mode will kill you when you get up on the numbers. So we look for—hope for—the shooter who is repeating the point numbers."

## 8. IF YOU ARE USING THE 5-COUNT TO INCREASE YOUR TIME AT THE TABLE FOR COMPING PURPOSES, WOULDN'T IT BE JUST AS EASY TO BET ON EVERY OTHER SHOOTER OR EVERY SHOOTER WHO IS TALL OR SHORT, OR SOME OTHER CRITERIA?

Yes, it would. But, betting every other shooter, or betting tall people or short people, or good looking people, or ugly people, is not the same as utilizing the *5-Count*. We aren't just using the *5-Count* to get more comps for less risk—that's a pleasant by-product of its utilization. We are using the *5-Count* because we are looking to save money in cold rolls so we have money to bet when the hot rolls come along. And the *5-Count* does eliminate crummy shooters for the most part, as I explained earlier.

Let's do a mind experiment to see how the *5-Count* differs from random selection of certain shooters. Let us take 10 shooters, one of which is going to have a good roll—say 30 point numbers in a row. We know this for a fact: That one of the 10 shooters is going to roll 30 point numbers without a 7. The problem is we don't know which one of the 10 shooters will have that good roll, just that one will. The other nine shooters are going to have rotten or mediocre rolls. Each of us gets to bet on five of the 10 shooters. You are going to select your five shooters randomly. I am going to use the *5-Count* (we assume for this mind experiment that the *5-Count* eliminates 50 percent of the shooters, which it often does in the real world of craps). Which one of us is guaranteed to be on the hot shooter? Obviously, it's me. You have a 50-50 chance to be on him based on a random selection. I have a 100 percent chance to be on him based on the *5-Count*.

Let us now speculate that we have 10 sets of 10 shooters (100 shooters in all, 10 hot ones total), all rolling 30 point numbers. You will be on five of the 10 shooters based on random selection as the probability is 50-50, but I will be on *every single one of them* based on the *5-Count*. You will actually win more on the five hot shooters you bet on since you are going up on them right away, while I'm not going up until the *5-Count* is completed. But I am on 10 of them, you are on five. I win a lot more money than you do. That's how the *5-Count* differs from random selection of shooters, or selecting tall or short, fat or skinny, well-dressed or undressed shooters merely to decrease your exposure to the house edge.

The *5-Count* is a direction finder, a guided missile, that looks to eliminate cold shooters—which it does beautifully as no one who doesn't make it through the *5-Count* is going to have a good roll because he's sevened out (as silly as that sounds, it is the truth)—and it positions us to take advantage of good shooters, who by definition must make it past the *5-Count* (again, silly-sounding but true).

Here's another mind experiment that you can do. Take all the shooters all over America who rolled the dice last week. Put the ones who sevened out before the *5-Count* was completed in one big arena and put the ones who made it through the *5-Count* in another big arena. Let's assume that 50 percent sevened out before the *5-Count* and 50 percent made it through the *5-Count* (and then sevened out whenever after). Which ones do you think you would have made money on? The arena with the shooters who didn't make it past the *5-Count* did not have one hot shooter in the bunch. The arena that holds the successful *5-Count* shooters had all the shooters who rolled for 20, 30, 40, 60 minutes or more. Which arena would you want to risk your money on? Precisely.

## 9. BUT THE REAL WORLD OF CRAPS PLAY IS NOT A MIND EXPERIMENT THAT YOU CAREFULLY ORCHESTRATE TO PROVE YOUR CONTENTIONS. HOW DOES THE 5-COUNT OPERATE IN THE REAL WORLD OF CASINO CRAPS?

You have "X" amount to bet. You can bet on every shooter one right after the other and hope that you hit a hot one before you run out of money, or you can use the *5-Count* and double or triple the number of shooters you get to see as the casino edge starts grinding away at you. If the shooters you run across in your small sampling are all strictly random rollers, you will merely last longer using the *5-Count*, get more in comps, and ultimately lose your bankroll. If there are occasional rhythmic rollers sprinkled among the multitudes, the longer you can hang in there before losing your stake, the better the chance that you'll be able to capitalize on those rhythmic rollers. This is not a complicated concept. In fact, the problem critics have with the *5-Count* is its simplicity. At the end of any prolonged series of craps sessions, where hundreds, if not thousands, of shooters have rolled them bones, you should be able in retrospect to see that the ones who sevened out before the *5-Count* would have lost you money and the ones who sevened out after the *5-Count* won you money or, at the very least, lost you less money. Indeed, the advantage-play method I am developing in this book is going to take the *5-Count* one step further than it's ever been taken before in an effort to eliminate as many *random* rollers as we possibly can, thereby giving us the best shot at those rare rhythmic rollers.

Apropos of the above, I received a letter from Mark Sanner on this very topic. Mark was asking how many average rolls the average shooter has. He wanted to ascertain what the likelihood of finding a hot shooter was. The *mathematical* likelihood. I sent Mark's letter over to University of Massachusetts's math professor Don Catlin, a gaming-math expert. Don did his usual detailed analysis and sent his calculations to Mark. Several days later Mark wrote Don and me a letter. (He also sent Don a nice mug for his efforts.) Here it is.

Dear Frank and Don,

After reviewing Don's calculations again, I was able to derive an answer to one important question: How long does a player have to wait to find a really hot shooter?

If I'm reading Don's Markov probability distribution table correctly, and we arbitrarily define a hot shooter as holding the dice for 40 rolls or more:

Probability of 40 rolls or more = 0.00378 ≥ 3.78 hot shooters per 1000 shooters ≥ 1 shooter in 265 will roll 40 or more.

So far so good, but how much time does it take to wade through 265 shooters? That depends on a number of factors, of course, but Erick St. Germain's "Craps System Tester" uses an average of about 0.9 minutes per roll. Since the average shooter has 8.5 rolls: 265 shooters x 8.5 rolls/shooter x 0.9 minutes/roll x 1 hour/60 minutes = 33.8 hours

In other words, on average, we can expect to have to spend about 34 hours at the table to find one really hot shooter. Of course all of these figures are approximate and subject to considerable variation, but suffice it to say that in a three-day weekend spending 10–12 hours per day at the tables (a lot of action, in my book), a player might expect to encounter only one really hot shooter.

Furthermore, the Captain's *5-Count* causes a player to wait at least five rolls before betting, and my sense from casino experience using the *5-Count* is that the average delay is more like six or seven rolls, or more than the calculated median of six rolls per shooter. That is, a *5-Count* player bets on fewer than half the shooters, on average, and although he's personally witnessed the "required" 265 shooters to find the one hot shooter, a *5-Counter* has risked money on fewer than 130 of them.

My view of the *5-Count* is that it effectively improves a player's batting average by preventing him from swinging at every pitch. A *5-Counter* is effectively betting to find one hot shooter in 130 or fewer rather than the usual 265 shooters. On the other hand, the "delayed entry" means that the player bets on perhaps only 33 or 34 rolls of a 40-roll hand, thereby reducing the size of the win: a mere 400 foot home run instead of a 500 footer. On balance, however, the gain realized by drastically reducing losses through *5-Counting* more than compensates for the somewhat smaller big wins.

This is, of course, exactly what Frank has been preaching for years, and I believe Don's calculations provide at least some support for this approach to the game. Don, if you haven't done so already, you might want to calculate the average number of rolls a player waits before betting using the *5-Count* (or *4-Count* or *3-Count* or *6-Count*). Referring this average to your Markov distribution table will tell us the approximate percentage of hands are actually in play using the *5-Count*.

The *5-Count* has been a great bankroll stretcher for me, but I've only been using it since last November, playing about twice per week. That's not a very large sample, though, so ask me again in five years how I feel about *5-Counting*.

Best regards,
Mark Sanner


Don Catlin and I are going to do a detailed analysis of the *5-Count* in an upcoming book. We'll look at it from every conceivable angle and let you know what we find. However, at this point, I think it is clear that using the *5-Count* can't hurt you, it can only help you. With apologies to Sam Grafstein, the original "dice doctor," if you think of a gaming author as Chance's physician then this particular physician abides by the Hippocratic oath: "Do no harm." If you play the *5-Count* exactly as I've outlined, I know that as your physician I have done you "no harm" and may have helped to keep your bankroll healthy in the bargain.

## 10. IF THE 5-COUNT IS SO OBVIOUSLY GREAT, WHY DON'T MORE PEOPLE PLAY IT?

Rudi Schiffer, the host of the weekly *Goodtimes Radio Show* in Memphis, a show devoted to the Tunica gaming experience, said to me on the air: "I know your books sell millions [a slight overstatement] but I have never seen a single person play the *5-Count* in Tunica and I'm in the casinos all the time. So how come?"

I replied: "Rudi, I've hung out with the Captain and his Crew and of 22 of them only the Captain and the late Jimmy P. played the *5-Count*. And the Crew are people who have seen the Captain in action, have witnessed his wins, who know that every word I've written about him is the truth—and they know all this from firsthand experience. So how come they don't play the *5-Count*? How come when I talk to them about the Crazy Crapper bets and how the casinos are extracting a ton of money from them because of their steady diet of these bets, they continue to make them? Some of the Crew members bet purple chips and bet black on the Crazy Crapper bets."

There was a long pause on the air. Not a good thing when you're on radio where "words, words, words" (to quote Hamlet) are the coin of the realm.

"Well," said Rudi at last, "Are you going to tell us why?"

"I don't really know," I said.

But I can certainly guess. Maybe it's the fact that people want to get into the action and there can be a lot of inaction when you play the *5-Count*. When you play the *5-Count* you can literally watch the dice go from shooter to shooter, even make a circuit of the whole table, without you ever getting in the game. Of course, when this is happening you're champing at the bit to get into the action—despite the fact that you have saved a bundle of money by not betting all those horrendous shooters. The Captain's Crew is composed of "action" players who bet wildly and have a great time. They aren't really in it to make a ton of money, just to have a ton of fun. To me, to the Captain, to other dedicated *5-Counters*, winning is the most fun, but obviously to many craps players, while they claim winning is why they play, their actions belie their words.

The *5-Count* is not for everyone. Indeed, I have received letters from people telling me that I am taking all the fun out of craps by suggesting that they play such a method. Some critics, not content to just ignore the Captain's advice, decide that I am "a brain-dead moron" for advocating such play, and that "the Captain" (they always put "the Captain" in quotation marks) is not a real person but a character I have made up.

The bottom line, gentle reader, is this: The *5-Count* either works or it doesn't work in the real world of casinos just as I've written it. You either play it or you don't. That's your choice. In truth, it is better for those of us who play it to have no one else play it so that we can go largely unnoticed.

You might be asking yourself this question right now: Why does Scoblete write so many books and articles extolling this method of play if he prefers that not many people play it? Why not just keep it a big fat secret? Three reasons really: 1. Human nature being what it is and most casino gamblers being what they are, the disparity of casino players who don't read anything at all to those who do read a book or two is gigantic—so it *remains* (more or less) a big, fat secret despite the fact that my books and tapes are on the shelves of bookstores all over the country. 2. The disparity of those who read gaming books to those who actually apply the methods they read about is just as immense. And, 3. As Billy Crystal said in *Throw Mama from the Train*: "A writer writes."

FOUR

# Step #2: How to Become a Rhythmic Roller

W hat do the Loch Ness Monster, Bigfoot, and Rhythmic Rollers (dice controllers) at craps have in common? The answer is that they are all relatively modern mythological creatures that have caught the fancy of the public—with Nessie and Bigfoot capturing the imagination of the monster hunters, and the Rhythmic Roller capturing the imaginations of craps players hunting for that monster roll.

These three myths may also share something else in common— there might be an element of truth in them. Many scientific expeditions, including one funded by *The New York Times*, have come to the conclusion that something is going on in the Loch, and certainly a whole industry has been constructed around hunting for Bigfoot in the great Northwest where otherwise credible people swear they have seen and scented the smelly beast. Of course, for everyone who merits these monsters with reality, there are scores of skeptical scientists who dismiss these creatures as fanciful remnants of a world long gone; a world inhabited by dragons, gorgons, gods, and ghosts. To the skeptical inquirer, science has slain the seance, math has murdered myth.

Likewise the notion that some shooters can control the dice thereby offsetting the casinos' mathematical edge at craps has some adherents and scores of detractors. The cons state that the math of craps is inviolable, which is true. In theory, craps is a negative expectation game (definition: the player loses in the long run) that falls into the *independent-trial* category—that is, what happened on the last decision has no influence on the next decision. The fact that the 7 just rolled four consecutive times does not increase or decrease its one-in-six chance of being rolled again.

Contrast this with the *dependent-trial* category of games such as blackjack where what happened on the last decision definitely affects what happens on the next. A single-deck blackjack game where all four aces come out in the first round is guaranteed not to have a fifth ace appear on the second round of play, unless something fishier than what's in Loch Ness is going on.

I asked the Captain to comment on the possibility of people controlling the dice. He is a firm believer that some people do indeed have the ability to alter the math of the game to favor the players. The Captain believes that there are two kinds of rhythmic rollers, "Those who do it consciously and those who do it unconsciously. The math of the game is based on the independent-trial model but the *physical reality* of the game is not. After all, shooters pick up the dice and roll the dice. Some shooters have learned either by practicing at home or in a casino to physically control the dice to a greater or lesser degree. They consciously have accomplished this. Others have stumbled upon a successful way to roll through an evolutionary process of trial and error; these are unconscious rhythmic rollers. I compare dice control to pitching in baseball. It's a physical ability that some people can develop."

The Captain believes the fact that a pitcher pitched a strike on the last pitch does not guarantee the outcome of the next pitch. "Pitching a baseball is an independent-trial event, just like craps, but it is also an event that has a physical dimension—just like craps. Rhythmic rolling is not absolute, it's more probabilistic, just like pitching. You don't know with certainty what the outcome will be on the next roll, but you know that based on your past experiences you have a much better chance of throwing certain combinations than other combinations. The pitcher is attempting to throw more strikes than balls and the good pitchers usually do. But the last pitch is no predictor of the success or failure to achieve a strike on the next pitch unless the batter is being intentionally walked. A rhythmic roller is merely trying to reduce the appearance of the 7 or increase the appearance of other numbers. Just like everyone who's thrown a ball will not have the talent to be a major league pitcher, not everyone who picks up the dice will be able to control them. It's not an easy task to master. If it was, the casinos would go broke or change the rules."

No fear on that first count, the casinos are not going broke at craps, but they are aware that some people do have the ability to control the dice. Indeed the modern craps table was built to thwart would-be rhythmic rollers by placing foam-rubber pyramids on the inner walls. Shooters must hit the opposite wall with both dice when they shoot. The pyramids then act as a physical randomizer that will make the actual game more in keeping with the mathematical model.

Still shooters can compensate for those pyramids as rhythmic roller Madeliene Bizub, who has gained quite a reputation for herself in Mississippi craps circles, explained to me: "After reading your books about craps, I must admit to a fair amount of skepticism relating to the rhythmic-rolling theory of the Captain and yourself. [But], if the results were random anyway, what could it hurt? So I set aside a special part of my gambling stake for just practicing different rolls, until I found one I was comfortable with. I discovered that I preferred the position to the right of the stick, on 12–14 foot tables. I had noticed that in that position, I could aim more easily for that little place at the bottom of the pyramids, down in the corner, and with careful aim I could get the dice to hit down there, and bounce just once, and not be skittering all over the table, or hitting chips, or flying off the table. My main goal was just to get them down there without flinging them all over the place.

"I practiced different ways of rolling. I set them [with the 3-spots] in the 'V' with the two and eight showing on the front dice, and the 'V' on top—that nasty little seven, not showing at all. I don't use much velocity, thus my table position choice, and I place the two dice between my thumb and index finger, and just lightly throw them down there, with very little arc, keeping them at eye level.

"When I first started doing that, it was heralded with many jeers and laughs from players and crew alike. Almost immediately after I started throwing the dice that way, I started having effective rolls—

very effective! I enjoyed how quickly the tone of the joking would change when I started making point after point [and having] 15–20 minute rolls almost every time."

Madeliene continues to have good rolls and some great rolls, although she has cooled off somewhat which is to be expected. After all, even Nolan Ryan didn't strike out every batter he faced.

Interestingly enough, Madeliene's husband, Larry Green, also seems to have the touch: "I do believe that I may be able to alter the randomness slightly. I seem to accomplish this by setting the dice the same way each time, throwing with the same velocity, and hitting the same spot. I've noticed this has given me similar results enough times that I certainly entertain the notion that I may be doing something that creates the outcome. My method is to set the 3-spots in a 'V' facing me, with the 6:2 combo up and the 5:1 combo down. I roll the dice with some gentleness, very low on the table. I'm left handed, and I like to stand at the far end with the entire length of the table in front of me. I get a lot of repeating sixes and eights, much more than the math calls for."

Of course, anecdotal stories do not prove the case for rhythmic rolling. A skeptic might say that such stories only prove that the people telling them are lying or have simply been experiencing a fluctuation of good luck. While one person's anecdotal evidence might hold up in a court of law ("Yes, I saw that man over there steal money!"), that same person's evidence is not automatically believed in the court of scientific opinion ("Yes, I saw Bigfoot right there beside my camper!"), or in the arena of gambling ("I can control the dice enough to change craps into a positive expectation game!").

Certainly not everyone who attempts to control the dice will succeed as the Captain noted. The combination of physical dexterity and concentration necessary to effectively alter the game of craps through physical means might be relatively rare. Still, is no one capable of such a feat as skeptics maintain? There is always a tendency on the part of people who can't do a thing to maintain that other people also can't do that thing. The Captain says: "The fact that a skeptic can't hit a baseball 500 feet doesn't mean that Mark McGwire can't do it."

Let us grant for argument's sake that some individuals who practice their rolls and are cognizant of their results are able to subtly alter the game to favor them. They have, after all, made a conscious effort to do so and they have succeeded. But how does someone become an "unconscious" rhythmic roller? Doesn't that strain credulity a bit too much?

"No," states the Captain. "Often physical mannerisms or traits are acquired unconsciously through a cause and effect relationship. A person starts to put the two 3s in a 'V' formation and has a good roll. Then the next time he's passed the dice, he has another decent roll using that same formation. The third time he's passed the dice, you can bet he'll set that 'V.' As long as his future results tend towards the positive end of the spectrum, he'll continue to set the dice the same way and attempt to roll the same way. He may not even be fully conscious of what he's doing. It becomes a habit. As long as the 'V' formation has been reinforced by success, even intermittent success, he'll keep doing it. Not everyone who sets the dice will become a rhythmic roller, of course, but no one—and I mean no one—who doesn't set the dice and take care with his rolls will."

Indeed, I have undergone a gradual evolution in my thinking from being a total skeptic grounded in mathematical craps theory before I met the Captain to being a believer in rhythmic rolling as I pen this chapter. A combination of factors converted me over time. Rhythmic rolling is a way to explain the efficacy of the Captain's *5-Count* methods of play. If even a small percentage of people are controlling the dice, the *5-Count* is the best possible way to locate them.

But other factors weighed in heavily as well. Having witnessed the success of the "Arm"—a member of the Captain's Crew and the first rhythmic roller I ever saw (I wrote about her in *Beat the Craps Out of the Casinos: How to Play Craps and Win!*)—to having had consistently good rolls for the past several years myself; to having more and more players telling me that they have been having success with the 3-spots 'V' sets I discussed in my audio cassette; and, finally, having encountered a remarkable young man who calls himself *Sharpshooter* and who leads a team of players who have hit the casinos for substantial amounts of money in the past half decade—I am a believer.

The Sharpshooter first wrote me a letter where he discussed his general ideas and experiences: "I visit the casinos some 50 to 60 times a year, and yes, I document my play. I have enough statistical proof to put me in the 99.99-plus percent confidence range. I also have slow-motion videos of my throw where you can see exactly how the dice are reacting. I have half of a craps table set up in my dining room where I practice about 45 minutes a day. What do I practice? A consistent delivery system.

"I work on my dice presets, my carefully balanced grip, and soft release. The dice go through identical motions hitting the table flat, and then taking what I call a 'dead cat bounce' up just grazing the rubber pyramids and coming down to rest. Can you control the dice 100 percent? No, but with practice you certainly can influence the dice 10 or 12 percent. If you make the more intelligent wagers on the table, you can easily overcome the thin house edges."

In a subsequent letter to my magazine *The New Chance and Circumstance*, Sharpshooter outlined his methods of attack and why they are successful. "In games where the motion of a pair of small cubes determines the outcome of that independent trial, you have to look at the rudimentary physics involved. Once you realize that this is a kinematics problem first, then the math does fall into place. For random shooters for every 36 tosses, on average (6) sevens; (5) sixes; (5) eights; (4) fives; (4) nines; (3) fours; (3) 10s; (2) twos; (2) 11s; (1) two, and (1) 12 would occur. This is about as far as the 'mathematical experts' of the game will take it. They have given absolutely no credence whatsoever to laws that govern rigid body translation and rotation, conservation of energy, angles of incidence and reflection, etc. It is for these and other reasons that I believe craps to be the *most beatable* game in the casino."

Sharpshooter continued: "At this point allow me to introduce a term that I refer to as Sevens-to-Rolls Ratio or SRR for short. This is simply the average number of tosses it takes for one seven to appear. For the above example (random), the SRR is 1:6, or for every six rolls on average, one will be a seven. Because there are two distinctly different directives in the game of craps, we need two SRR's. On the Come Out roll, we set for and shoot for the sevens; hopefully this SRR is less than 1:6 producing a higher frequency of sevens. During the point cycle, where we try to elude the sinister seven, we have a SRR that is greater than 1:6 for lower seven frequency. This second SRR is the chief SRR that I will be referring to herein. For a well practiced dice mechanic this SRR may be as high as 1:8.

"For the past three years of documented play, my personal SRR is 1:7.83. This may not sound impressive but it is statistically significant. One of the shooters on my team is currently holding an SRR just shy of 1:9. This is for 5,000+ recorded trials over six months. Lately we've been giving him his favorite position and trying to talk other players into passing the dice directly over to him.

"Let's look at a frequency distribution for a shooter with an SRR of 1:7. For every 36 tosses, (5) sevens will occur.

"Because the frequency of sevens thrown has been reduced by physical means, the remaining numbers will increase to fill in the void. I've calculated the percent edge for various craps wagers at different SRR skill levels. I'll include a subset to make my point (no pun intended).

"For the six or eight place bet with a random shooter, you will have (6) sevens for every (5) sixes or eights. You are paid $7 for a $6 bet which translates into a house edge of 1.515 percent. For the 1.7 SRR skilled player, you will get (5) sevens for every (5) sixes or eights. You are paid $7 for $6 bet which translates into a 8.333 percent edge— for the player!

"The SRR needed to break even on placing the six or eight is 1:6.143. A 2.326 percent influence is all that is needed to break even for the six or eight place bet. You do not need to 'control' the dice to profit at craps. All that is needed is a minute amount of influence. Because the house edge is smaller on the Pass Line bet as compared to the six or eight place bet, a shooter with an SRR of 1:6.143 will make modest sums if he makes Pass Line with odds. Imagine how much havoc a shooter with a 1:8 or even a 1:7 SRR can wreak!"

I met Sharpshooter in Las Vegas several months later, just after his team had finished a successful week-long attack on the downtown casinos. Indeed, the team was successful, but Sharpshooter himself had come in for some heavy hazing at a downtown casino for his remarkable *good luck*. "By the end of my play, the stickmen were constantly holding the stick out to prevent me from arcing the dice as I usually do and then the boxman would yell at me if I didn't hit the back wall. It was a very bad experience."

You know there's something to the idea of "advantage play" when the casinos take counter measures against the advantage player. In blackjack, it is customary at some casinos to ask skilled players to leave. Indeed being asked to leave a casino is almost a rite of passage for some blackjack players and certain Vegas casinos have become veritable blackjack baptismal fonts for novices wishing to be baptized into the card counting fraternity.

And the same holds true for the small but growing numbers of rhythmic rollers at craps. Some casinos are beginning to change the nature of the game and the rules. For example, the Captain's *Supersystem* has been barred from play at John Ascuaga's Nugget in

Sparks, Nevada; Resorts in Atlantic City, New Jersey; Binions in Louisiana and Fitzgeralds in Tunica, Mississippi, among others, according to individuals who attempted to play it at these places.

Indeed, several rhythmic rollers I interviewed preferred that I use pseudonyms, although Bizub and Green did not. One rhythmic roller was adamant: "I don't want my name revealed. I'm a high roller and even though I was betting substantial amounts, [the casino] told me that I was welcome to play as long as I didn't roll or play the Supersystem, but if I attempted to I'd be asked to leave."

Here is a letter I received from T.G. about his experiences in craps trying to rhythmically roll:

Dear Frank:
I have been enthralled by the prospects of rhythmic rolling for a while now, and have been practicing at home ardently. I came up with a good placement and grip, and felt very comfortable after many hours of practice. After reading your story on rhythmic rolling in *Chance Magazine*, I decided it was time to give my technique a try in the "real world." I live in South Lake Tahoe and ventured to Bill's Casino recently for a go at the craps tables.

After betting conservatively while the dice made their way around the table, my time had finally come to throw. I laid my modest Pass Line bet, grabbed the cubes appropriately, and expertly tossed them down the table. They hit the surface, took a small bounce against the back wall, and died just the way I had practiced for and planned on; they landed on the 8. To make a long story short, I hit my point twice within the first five rolls, and people began making their way around my table to watch.

After I had hit my second point, the stickman began giving me a hard time. I threw again and nailed the 8 again. When he pushed the bones in front of me, he informed me that I could no longer grip them the way I wanted. He told me I had to grab them and throw them in one motion. I again clutched them as I had previously and threw them to another 8. He pushed them back to me and told me that if I did it again, he would have me thrown out of the casino or arrested! I grabbed them and threw them like any other person and sevened out.

My question is simple. Do the craps dealers have the right to tell me how to throw, or was he just being a jerk and trying to rattle me? Please let me know how people get away with rhythmic rolling, and please let me know if it is like this at all casinos.
Thank you for your time.
T.G.

I answered T.G. somewhat hastily and lambasted the dealer for indeed being a jerk. In fact, a huge controversy erupted over the

Internet concerning my response to T.G. In truth, the dealer might not have been a jerk but was, instead, probably just following house rules. Or T.G. might not have yet developed his dice set and delivery smoothly enough to cause no break in the action. No matter. The fact that casinos evince such concern means that there is probably something to be concerned about. The key to rhythmic rolling, or rather, getting away with rhythmic rolling, is to do it swiftly and surely . . . and to tip the dealers before you start. Even a small Hardways bet for the dealers will get them on your side. The stickman will then be somewhat more reluctant to hassle you.

## The Three Principles of Rhythmic Rolling

So what is involved in getting the dice to obey your will?

1. *A shooter must set the dice a specific way and usually shoot from a specific spot.* I use the 3-spots in a 'V' or pyramid shape and place my thumb at the base of the pyramid and my index and middle finger at the peak. My preferred location is to the stickman's immediate right. Not everyone will find this a comfortable set or a comfortable position to play. I am also practicing at "low-limit" tables to achieve the good results from other spots at the table since you can't always get next to the stickman.

2. *The shooter must develop a consistent delivery* as Sharpshooter and the Captain stress. I try to hit the back wall at the spot just before it curves (the curve nearest me) so that the dice do one hop and die quickly without much bouncing. As the dice make their journey they are close together and hopefully they hit the wall side by side and stop. I want the 3-spots to stay face up. (At Binions Horseshoe, I once hit nine Hardways in a row—six of them the hard 6!)

3. *A player must recognize that his control is not absolute* and that he shouldn't bet foolishly on the hope that his next roll will be a monster.

## Understanding Dice Sets

I am not an expert in rhythmic rolling, despite the fact that I have been having excellent rolls for several years now; I am only an expert in *my* rolling technique. There may be better ones than mine. [In fact, Sharpshooter himself is writing a book for my "Frank Scoblete Get-the-Edge Guides" at Bonus Books titled, appropriately enough, *Get the Edge at Craps: How to Control the Dice!*] However, a close analysis of my own technique will help us to understand why it works as it does.

When I set the dice in the "V" or pyramid formation with my thumb at the base of the pyramid and my index and middle finger at the point of the pyramid, all adjoining dice faces are either 6 or 8—the two most common numbers after the dreaded 7. The 4:4 is on the bottom; while one adjoining side will show a 6-spot and a 2-spot and the other adjoining side will show a 5-spot and a 1-spot; on opposite sides to the left and right will be found the 6-spot and the 2-spot. A second dice set with the "V' shape sees the 4:4 again at the bottom; with adjoining sides containing a 2-spot and a 1-spot; and a 5-spot and a 6-spot, with and the 2-spot and the 1-spot on opposite sides to the left and right. You will note that there are no 7s on adjoining dice when they are set either way.

## How to Roll Dem Bones

Once I've set the dice, my goal is to gently loft them to my spot just before the wall curves. As Madeliene Bizub said, I don't want them bouncing, careening, or ricocheting all over the place. I want them to land close to the wall, hit softly, and die on the spot. When I loft them, I try to keep them together in the air so that they land touching each other. This seems to help them die more quickly than when they are apart. I also think keeping them close together helps them stay on the 3-spots more than they normally would. In fact, that is my ultimate goal, having one die (or both dice) maintain the 3-spot intact. Why is this important? Because if one die can be a 3, even a small percentage of the time—but a larger percentage than normal!—I have just changed the nature of the game in my favor.

Here's why:

The normal 36 combinations of two six-sided dice will now be skewed because the 3-spot coming up more frequently than 1:6 on one die causes a ripple effect—it diminishes the appearance of the 4-spot proportionally and it decreases the appearance of the 10 in combination. (Remember that you can't make a 10 with a 3-spot!) Let us say that in two rolls of this die, instead of the 3-spot coming up 2 in 12 as probability would indicate, it came up, say, three times. The first implication would be the 4-spot on the reverse side would only come up once in 12 rolls, as opposed to its normal twice in 12 rolls. The numbers that could be made with a 3-spot would increase; the numbers that could be made with a 4-spot would decrease. The number 4 would appear slightly more often; the number 10 slightly less often.

Is this exactly how it has worked out for me? I don't know. Since I don't really keep track of the numbers when I'm rolling (writing them down would break my rhythm), I have to rely on memory. The numbers I seem to hit when I roll are 4, 6, and 8. I do know that in the past few years of playing—and I have played a lot—I am consistently winning money on myself. I am not always having monster rolls. I rarely have monsters. Rarely does anyone have monsters. But I am having rolls where I hit a bunch of numbers and come out ahead. For the other shooters, the *5-Count* has done its job. I rarely get blown away in craps anymore.

One of the best descriptions of rhythmic rolling was sent to me by someone who calls himself The Midnight Skulker. It was published in *The New Chance and Circumstance* magazine (Issue #22, Fall 1999). The Midnight Skulker is a frequent poster to Internet craps news groups and he obviously has given this considerable thought.

He contends that rhythmic rolling "combines dice setting with one of three main categories of deliveries, which are presented in ascending order of potential for control. In general that potential increases as the difficulty of the technique increases, hence *rolling* is the easiest technique to perform with some efficiency and *lobbing* is the most difficult.

"Precision *rollers* try to roll the dice so that they tumble forward only (i.e. with no sideways rotation), strike the wall, and bounce straight back (again with no sideways rotation). If successfully executed, this technique keeps two faces of each die, the ones on the sides, from showing thereby reducing the number of possible combinations from 36 to 16. In addition this subset of 16 combinations can be varied depending on the situation (to favor 7 on the Come Out roll for example).

"*Stackers* throw the dice trying to keep one die on top of the other so that they land close to (ideally at the base of) the wall. When this technique is successfully executed the top die will freeze the bottom die showing whatever number it was set to when the dice were tossed thereby reducing the number of possible combinations from 36 to six. As with precision rolling this subset of six combinations can be varied as desired.

"*Lobbers* throw the dice side by side trying to keep both of them from rotating at all while in flight so that when they land at the base of the wall they bounce against the bottom of the back row of pyramids and come to rest immediately with both dice showing whatever numbers they were set to when they were tossed. In theory this reduces the number of possible combinations from 36 to one, the combination the dice were set to when they were tossed, which of course can be varied as desired; in practice, however, even the best lobber is ecstatic if the dice turn in concert one or more faces forward or backward (not sideways), which makes four combinations possible."

Naturally, in the best of all possible worlds you wouldn't have to worry about the dice hitting someone's chips, nor would you have deal with the stickman's belly or stick hanging over the table if you selected the position to his right as I do. But in the real world all these factors, and others, can interfere with your attempts to control the dice. That's why even if rhythmic rolling is fact and not a supposition—and I do believe it is a fact—it is also a fact that even the best rhythmic roller is only going to have slight control, enough to switch a slightly negative game into a slightly positive mode. Do not expect, even if you do develop a good roll, to win every time you roll the bones. As the Captain says: "Even the very best pitcher in baseball does not throw strikes on every pitch; he does not strike out every batter and he does not win every game. The best rhythmic rollers just win somewhat more than they lose and this puts them in the plus category."

## Temporary Rhythmic Rollers

Veteran craps players have seen the following scenario a thousand times. A shooter is on a hot roll. He's like a machine. The stickman gives him the dice with anything but the 7 showing on their combined faces. He picks up the dice, lobs the dice, the dice hit and land on anything but the 7 on their combined faces. The shooter's face has that faraway look, as if he's in a trance. A rolling trance. This continues for five, ten, 15 minutes. Then some obnoxious guy sidles next to him and says "How're ya doin?" The shooter comes out of a dream and says: "Fine, fine, I'm having a good roll." The obnoxious guy pushes his way onto the table and makes room for himself by elbowing the shooter a little to get himself comfortable. Then he throws a wad of bills on the table: "Give me a twelve dollar 6 and 8." The dealer does as requested but when the obnoxious guy gets his change back he says: "Now, give me an 11, a Hard 8 and a Hard 4, and a . . . yeah, give me a 10." All the while he's throwing chips on the table as if he's a big shot. The shooter has started to talk to the guy next to him on the other side. Finally, after what seems like ages, the dice are ready to be put into the shooter's hot hands. He picks them up (differently), he throws them (differently), and they land (differently) to a booming "Seven! Seven-out!" of the stickman. The obnoxious guy curses the shooter and storms off. He should have cursed himself.

States the Captain: "I certainly do believe there is such a thing as a temporary rhythmic roller. Someone who gets in a groove and for however long it lasts is changing the percentages."

The Captain does not believe that everyone who has a hot roll is a temporary rhythmic roller, however. Far from it. He estimates that maybe one or two percent of hot rolls, defined as those rolls that last for 10 to 15 minutes, will be caused by this phenomenon. "You could shoot the dice out of a small cannon and there will be a number of good rolls just because of randomness. But in the real world, every so often, you see the temporary rhythmic roller in action. They have that mesmerized look. They roll like a machine. They exist in their own world."

You also see the things that destroy their world, such as the obnoxious player barging in and elbowing them, or the casino hauling out the chip trays and placing them on the table right in the line of fire, or the temporary rhythmic roller's wife or girlfriend (or husband or boyfriend) asking him (or her) how he (or she) is doing. This throws his rhythm off, causes him to change his delivery, and ultimately makes him just another random roller. Seven-out!

"Sometimes," says the Captain, "the temporary rhythmic roller alters his throw himself. He might be getting cocky. Now, instead of picking up the dice a certain way, he decides to get fancy. He might pick them up, then put them down, then pick them up again and change the order of the dice faces. No apparent reason, just to be cool. He breaks his own rhythm. He will not even realize it but he does it and it ends his temporary rhythmic roll. Or, he'll start calling out his point, when before he just concentrated on his roll. You'll notice that when he starts to call out his point, he changes his delivery."

One of the great superstitions of dice concerns interfering with the shooter. The Captain believes that it has its roots in the temporary rhythmic roller. "It is a cardinal principle at the craps table that a hot roll will end when someone messes with the shooter. The origin of this superstition is, I believe, the rhythmic roller. Enough players over the years have seen this phenomenon of a shooter sevening out after he's been taken out of his rhythm so that gradually a superstition grew up about it."

And it is quite possible, perhaps likely, that the casino bosses share this belief as well.

# One Crew Member's View of "Messing with the Shooter"

The Captain has surrounded himself with Runyonesque characters as a part of his Crew. One such was the late Jimmy P., a jovial, generous and flamboyant mega-high roller. Of all the Captain's Crew only Jimmy P. was able to consistently play the Captain's methods—methods such as the *5-Count* which require great discipline, concentration and patience to employ. In fact, Jimmy had been at times a devastating presence in Atlantic City casinos utilizing these methods as witnessed by his winning upwards of a half million dollars in one 18 month stretch of playing two days a week with the Captain. Jimmy's idea of a five-dollar bet needed a couple of zeroes added before the decimal point to understand what a hot streak of his could do to the casino treasury. Wins (and losses) in the thousands and tens-of-thousands of dollars were nothing unique to this man who had won and lost more money in a given week than many people make in a given year.

What was unique, however, was Jimmy's willingness to believe some of the more enduring superstitions or myths in the world of craps. I am not talking about such superstitions as never saying the word "seven" at a table for fear that the dice will hear you and come up with that dreaded number, or believing that a player throwing his money down when the dice are in flight will cause a seven to appear should the dice brush the bills, or believing that dangling your hands over the side where the dice can hit them will also bring on the seven, or believing that you must ask for the "same dice" when the dice go off the table in the belief that the "new dice" will cause the 7 to appear as well.

No, Jimmy was the conspiracy theorist of the Captain's Crew who firmly believed that the casinos purposely tried to disrupt a rhythmic roller's concentration in order to end potentially great rolls. "You don't think the casinos know how to screw up a good roll from a good shooter? I seen it a million times. How many times you see a shooter on a hot roll get jerked around by the pit? The pit guy says: 'Make sure you hit the back wall, sir,' if the shooter misses with one dice one time. They know that the shooter's got to put a little more force the next time and that can disrupt the guy's rhythm.

"In some casinos all of a sudden out of nowhere they'll tell a guy on a hot roll that he can't fix the dice before he throws them. He's been fixing the dice every roll for a half hour but now he can't fix them no more! Then they push the dice over to him with the 7 showing and at the last minute they flip one of them so it isn't the 7. Or they push the dice to him and as he's about to reach and take them, they drag the dice back for some phony reason. All this is to upset the guy's rhythm, and his mind, and screw up his roll.

"Then on really hot rolls they decide they got to bring over the chip tray and replace the chips in the racks. They interrupt the game and all these chip trays are put on the table while the shooter is cooling his heels and maybe cooling off. Then they start to stack the chips but now they want the shooter to shoot anyway—sometimes the shooter's got to shoot around the chip trays they have on the table. I seen that a hundred times over the years. They got plenty of chips. They don't need refills just at that moment. It's done to disrupt the shooter.

"Or, they come over and want to ask for your name or for your card just as you get set to roll the dice again or they ask if you want a comp—right in the middle of your roll. They figure you get out of your rhythm that way when you have to divert your attention from shooting. Or they invite a new player to the table and purposely point to the spot next to the shooter so that the shooter has to move a little. I seen these things done all the time. Or if the dice do go off the table and the shooter asks for the same dice, the boxman takes a month to examine the dice—like he was performing brain surgery. Then he flips the dice down and the stickman sometimes tries to get new dice in or make it look like he's getting new dice in in order to have the shooter say: 'Hey, I want the same dice.' The more you screw around with a shooter during a great roll, the better chance you have to disrupt his rhythm and his concentration. I hate it when casinos screw around with the shooters."

Of course, I have experienced all the things that Jimmy P. has pointed out but I don't know if each and every one of them is designed to disrupt the shooter, be he a rhythmic roller or just hot. But plenty of players—not just Jimmy P.—think casinos do this. It is a wise pit boss who tells his floorpeople, boxmen and dealers, to make sure they never "screw around" with the shooters on a hot roll. Messing with the shooter might win some money for the casino when he sevens out but it might also lose some customers when they leave in a huff and take their business elsewhere.

# The Professor Takes a Quick Look

Finally, I asked Dr. Don Catlin, professor of mathematics at the University of Massachusetts, to do some preliminary work on rhythmic rolling to see how much of a change in the house edge certain combinations could accomplish. He e-mailed me his response:

Dear Frank:

Here are the results of my calculations. If one could increase the probability of the left die showing a 6-spot by just 25 percent then the probability of the 6-spot would become 5/144 and the probability of the 1-spot would drop to 3/144; all of the other number-spots would be 1/6 as before. Using these numbers the probability of the sum drops for 2 through 6 and increases for 8 through 12. The net result is that the straight Pass Line has a slight advantage for the player of 0.05 percent. However, if this player takes double odds on the 8, 9, and 10 the edge to the player per Pass Line decision rises to 2.62 percent. The average bet in this case is 1.71 so the edge to the player is 1.53 percent per unit risked.

Sharpshooter claims to be able to decrease the probability of a 7 to 1/7.83. According to him the other numbers increase proportionally. I worked this out and got the following probabilities:

$p(2) = p(12) = 0.029076202$
$p(3) = p(11) = 0.058152405$
$p(4) = p(10) = 0.087228607$
$p(5) = p(9) = 0.116304810$
$p(6) = p(8) = 0.145381013$
$p(7) = 0.127713920$

I assumed that on the Come Out roll no attempt was made to control the 7 so the usual dice probabilities applied. If a point was established then I used the above numbers. The Pass Line bet returns a 9.90 percent return to the player. If, in addition, the player just takes single odds this number is increased by 12.64 percent to 22.53 percent. The average bet when single odds are taken is 1 2/3 units so multiplying the last number by 3/5 we get a player advantage of 13.52 percent per unit risked.

It seems clear that even a much smaller decrease in the frequency of the 7 would turn this game in the player's favor. Notice that in the scenario above, the 6 and 8 are more likely than the 7 so placing the 6 and 8 is undoubtedly a good bet.

Hope this is of some help.

Regards,

Don

# Practice Makes Imperfect

The only way for anyone to become a rhythmic roller is to practice. Most players can't afford a craps table to put in our basements or play rooms. Some of us might not have the room for such a thing. For those of us who can't practice at home, the only practice we are going to get is in the actual world of casino play. That's fine. Chances are you are playing already, rolling them bones already, and putting your money at risk already. If you really want to spend a lot of time at the tables practicing your rolls, the morning is the best time. Tables are empty, minimums are low. Put a Pass Line bet for the minimum and practice. Don't bother placing odds. You're just practicing your rolls. If you are a green chip or black chip player, taking an hour or so each day at a three-dollar or five-dollar table to practice your technique will not cost you very much. You might want to have a friend or a spouse record the dice faces that come up on your rolls so that you can go over your progress at your leisure. The pit won't care if someone is recording your numbers, they'll think it's some "systems" player and ignore you.

You'll want to work on presets, delivery, and table position. Some of you might find that, like me, you prefer to be as close to the back wall as possible so the dice have the shortest distance to travel. You might want to position yourself close to the stickman. Others might find that being at one end of the table gives a clear, unobstructed view of the "spot" where you want the dice to land. Even as I write this, I know that I must work on dice throws from positions other than to the immediate right of the stickman because on crowded tables I can't always have my spot.

If you are playing craps already, practicing in the real heat of the game can't possibly hurt you—after all, you're already playing. So the very next time you go to the casino should be for fun and practice . . . and practice . . . and practice. Remember that a rhythmic roller does not have to be perfect to effectively change a slightly negative game to a slightly positive game.

# Conclusion

Is rhythmic rolling a fact or is it still in the quasi-real–fantastical category of the Loch Ness Monster and Bigfoot? By way of analogy, here's my answer: A hundred years ago when missionaries in Africa reported that they were seeing huge hairy manlike beasts that were gargantuanly bigger than the chimpanzee, scientists mocked them. "There are no huge, hairy manlike beasts in the jungles," laughed the scientists. Several years later the first gorilla was discovered. In the rhythmic rolling controversy, I'm betting on the gorilla. After all, I've seen the hairy manlike thing with my own eyes!

# FIVE

# Step #3: The Golden Ruler

*L* *ook for in others what you expect from yourself.*

That's the golden rule of advantage-play craps. As the Captain has stated: "No one who doesn't take care with his shooting style is— or can be—a rhythmic roller. No one who doesn't make it through the *5-Count* can have an epic (or even good) roll." Combine those two facts and you have the one-two punch for craps play: Left (the *5-Count*), right (rhythmic rolling) = knockout!

But first a little background. My belief that craps could be overcome with a combination of *5-Counting* and rhythmic rolling evolved over time. It wasn't until the summer of 1998, during a month-long stretch of playing craps every day in Las Vegas, that I hit upon what I believe to be the key to getting the edge at an unbeatable game. Until that summer, I always hedged my bets by couching my craps writing in maybe's, perhaps, could be's, and mights. I had to recognize that the Captain was ahead of the game for almost two decades, and I had to recognize that some shooters (notably the "Arm" in

Atlantic City) "probably" controlled the dice and that this factor "probably" helped the Captain be ahead for that period of time, but for most players I had to realize that the game was still unbeatable owing to a combination of bad math, bad betting, and bad shooting. I had personally started using the "V" sets and positioning myself to the right of the stickman in 1995, from which time I started to be well ahead of the game on my own rolls. Finally, I decided to do a little experiment to see if maybe it was the combination of rhythmic rolling and *5-Counting* coupled with low house-edge bets that could turn the trick—and make me go from a person "willing to believe" in advantage-play craps to a person who actually did believe that craps could be beaten in this way in the long run. I turned the corner when I wrote the following article for my magazine *Chance and Circumstance* (Issue #18, Fall 1998).

*** 

# The 24 Golden Shooters

As readers of *Chance and Circumstance* know, I have become somewhat obsessed with the idea that certain shooters can control the dice. Like Mulder in The *X-Files*, "I want to believe!" I also know why I want to believe that some people have the ability to physically alter the odds at craps by the way they shoot the dice. It would help explain why the Captain has been successfully beating what should, by all mathematical standards, be an unbeatable game. It would explain why the *5-Count* works to set up the conditions for winning at a negative expectation game. It would explain why the Captain is so insistent that people take care with their rolls and not just fling the dice down the felt.

It would also help me personally to know that controlled dice throws—rhythmic rolling as the Captain calls it—are a reality and not just a wishful thought in my hopeful mind. I am the type of gaming writer who is grounded in the math of the games. I prefer that the math be correct not just theoretically, but in the real world. It is upsetting to think that the math might not actually be the be-all and end-all of every gambling game. The casinos, after all, go to the bank because of the math and that is a fact. (Yet, those very same casinos will hassle individuals who are taking care with their dice throws . . .

hmmm?) Advocating the idea that maybe, just maybe, craps can be beaten also opens me up to criticism from other writers who reject out-of-hand any notion that the real-world odds of the game of craps can be changed by shooters and that the *5-Count* is the way to ferret out such shooters. No one likes to be viewed as gullible. No one likes to be pictured as an idiot. Certainly I don't. Still, I have to be true to what I have personally experienced and not to some paradigm of gaming orthodoxy. I *know* the Captain has been beating craps for almost 20 years now! Not because I want to believe it but because I have seen it with my own eyes and, more importantly, I have confirmed it with casino executives in Atlantic City who have known the Captain and his Crew for all these years. One casino executive, now with the Trump organization, said this to me several years ago: "The Captain has been killing us for 12 years!" Tropicana (when it was Tropworld) sent out a memo about the Captain, explaining that while they couldn't figure out how he and Jimmy P. (one of his Crew) were doing it, both of these men had won substantial amounts of money ever since they started playing at the Tropworld Casino. The memo went on to state how the guys bet and warned other casinos in Atlantic City about them. How did I find out about the memo? Why a casino executive at Resorts showed it to the Captain and he showed it to me! I also know what I have done at craps for approximately 10 years now using the Captain's *5-Count* with the Supersystem and the traditional Pass/Come bets. Simply to deny what I have experienced because it doesn't fit the belief system of orthodox gaming writers would make me a coward and a liar. Of course, I can't do what the phony systems sellers do: I can't guarantee that this is a foolproof method and then charge exorbitant sums to learn it. Not everyone who has tried the *5-Count* has been successful. It might not be able to overcome, say, the Place betting odds for those who bet the five, nine, four and ten. I can't sell how to play the Captain's way for thousands of dollars in the cynical belief that people will gladly part with enormous sums because they think they get what they pay for. That might be true in some areas of the marketplace but it isn't true in gambling. The best systems, ideas, and methods of play usually don't cost more than the price of a book or tape. Certainly mine don't. Certainly none of the writers who write for *Chance and Circumstance* are selling high-priced systems and they are the best gaming writers in the country.

The preceding was merely preparatory to sharing with you a little experiment I did this past summer while I was in Las Vegas—an experiment designed not necessarily to prove conclusively whether people can control the dice or whether such things as rhythmic rollers exist, but one rather to tell me whether I should continue to flirt with the idea that such individuals exist or to shut my mouth and stop embarrassing myself with all this stuff about being able to overcome craps. As most of my readers know, my primary game is blackjack and while craps is the most enjoyable game to play, and the most exciting, I do not risk anywhere near the amount of money at craps as I do at blackjack where I can get a mathematical edge. (Math is the great comforter of astute gamblers after all. Even as they go bust, as many card counters do, an astute player will say: "At least I had the edge—not like those other fools!")

Here is what I did. I decided that I would bet on 24 shooters— one each day while I was in Vegas. The shooter I would risk money on had to achieve the *5-Count* and be taking great care with his roll. I would not bet any shooters who did not fix and set the dice and throw them the same way each time—even if such a careless shooter did make it past the *5-Count*. I would risk money on the safest mathematical bets—the traditional Pass and Come with the most I could afford in odds behind. I was willing to risk between $50 and $100 per shooter. I would do this with the least on the Pass/Come and the most I could take in odds behind.

However, since I was primarily interested in finding shooters and not in finding craps games with the best odds, there were games where I was risking $50 to $100 placing double odds and there were games where I was placing 20X odds. I usually tried to get up on three numbers when I was at risk but sometimes I didn't achieve that goal because the shooters sevened out relatively early after they had achieved the *5-Count*.

The idea behind the *5-Count* is simple. If a shooter succeeds in making it, he might be in a groove and about to have a good roll. Certainly no shooter who doesn't make it through the *5-Count* can have a good roll—because he has already sevened out! Of course, most shooters who actually make it through the *5-Count* don't have good rolls. You do lose money on them. However, you do not lose as much money as the poor schnook who has been betting on every single shooter and, hopefully, if and when the few hot shooters come along, you haven't lost so much money that you can't make it up and get into the black. That's the theory and that has been my experience of how it works in practice. The "why" it seems to work is a matter of conjecture—the Captain conjectures that rhythmic rollers are out there and that they change the nature of the game. I concur with his conjecture.

So I was specifically looking for the rollers who would prove the point to my satisfaction. In 24 shooters, carefully selected for their careful attempts to control the dice, would I be ahead, behind, even? Would I have fuel to continue toying with the idea that craps can be beaten by such shooters and the *5-Count* is the most ingenious way to find them? Or, would these shooters prove nothing? Naturally, 24 shooters does not a definitive study make. I know that. It would take many hundreds of shooters or, maybe just one shooter who could demonstrate a controlled throw time and again in a controlled environment.

If I felt the 24 shooters gave evidence that I was on the right track in assuming the math of craps can be altered by physical means then I would not hesitate to continue to flirt with this idea in my writing— even if it opened me up to more criticism from my fellow writers— friends and critics alike. For example, I can see Walter Thomason, Henry Tamburin and John Grochowski right now shaking their collective heads and saying: "Frank's usually on the money in his writing but he's totally demented with this craps control stuff! Poor guy, such a good mind going to the devil."

Well, hold your breath fellas because—I won money on every single one of the 24 shooters! I repeat. I did not lose on any shooter! Not one. Not one. Not once.

About a third of the shooters I won a single bet on. On the 4-count I would put up a Come bet (sometimes a Pass Line bet), the shooter would roll a point number, I'd go up on it, take odds, then the shooter would repeat that number and then seven out. I'd win on the come and once on the number. Not a big profit. Not a good roll. But just repeating one number won me a little money. Nine shooters were like this. (Say I had a Come bet of $5 on the 4-count and he rolls a six. Then I take $25 in odds because he's made it past the *5-Count*. I put up another Come bet. He rolls another six. I get a $30 return. Then he rolls a seven. I win on the Come $5. I won a total of $35 but I lost $30. A $5 win.)

Another third (actually seven) of the shooters had marginal rolls. I'd get up on a few numbers, they'd hit them but then seven out. So I'd have a small profit on them. The final third was divided between five good shooters and three *epic* shooters. The good shooters did not have long rolls but they did hit the numbers I was on several times each and I made a decent profit from them. The three epic shooters were 20, 30 to 40 minute rolls with repeating numbers. One was a guy at Sunset Station (20X odds with $3 minimum) who reminded me of some of the Captain's Crew. He was definitely from the Brooklyn of Tirty-turd street! He rolled for close to 30 minutes with one of the most carefully controlled throws I've ever seen. He sevened out when he became distracted by the ploppy next to him who patted him on the back just before he shot ("Yuch! Yuch! Keep it up!" said the ploppy patting him). The shooter paused and hesitated, then rolled and bang! seven-out! I made a lot of money on that shooter, however. A second good shooter was also at Sunset Station. This was a young man of about 30. He took care with his roll and he'd put the dice on top of each other. The top die would die when it hit the back wall. He rolled for 20 minutes.

The third shooter was a classic. This was at Bally's. He was also a relatively young man who set the dice with the two threes in a "V" as I do. He had a 40 minute roll. Although he hit a lot of garbage numbers—at one point he hit the craps numbers 2 and 3 five times in a row!—he hit so many numbers that by the time he was finished with his roll I was up on every number. But here's the beautiful kicker: When his lady friend came to the table and asked him how he was doing, I figured he was taken out of his rhythm and I called off all my odds. He rolled once and hit one of the numbers. But on the second roll after his lady friend came to the table, he sevened out. Except for the loss of the line bets, I got all my odds back. This was my best score of the summer.

There you have it. I do realize that this doesn't definitively prove anything. All it does is continue to fuel my growing belief (delusion?) in rhythmic rollers and in the soundness of the Captain's philosophy of craps. It also continues to put me at odds with the orthodoxy of gaming thinking—an orthodoxy I am a part of when it comes to all games except craps. Yes, the nine shooters who basically made me a tiny profit could just as easily have lost me money as could the seven shooters who hit a few of the few numbers I was on. That turnaround would not be hard—a single roll really. Still, even with that happening, with—say—me losing on 16 of those shooters, the eight shooters who had good or epic rolls would have made me come out ahead— way ahead.

So what does this tell me? First, it tells me to tell you, my readers, that you shouldn't take this little experiment of mine as proof that you should quit your job and become a professional craps player. No, no. That would be much too risky, much too foolhardy. But it does tell me to tell you to give careful selection of shooters a try. When you next play craps, use the *5-Count* but also look for shooters who are taking care with their rolls. Risk money only on them. Naturally, I was not playing a session; I was not looking to be comped; I was just looking for a single "golden shooter" in a single day. I had all day to discover the shooters I wanted. You might not have the luxury of that kind of time. After all, I was in the casinos playing blackjack already and all I had to do was walk through the craps pits looking for what I was looking for. And also keep this in mind: If rhythmic rollers are changing the odds, chances are they are only changing the odds a little. Despite the fact that I had an extraordinary run with my "golden 24" I wouldn't bet that number 25 would also make me money. Most times at craps you are behind, that's a fact. Then along comes a good shooter who, hopefully, puts you ahead. The purpose of the *5-Count* is to see to it that you aren't too much behind before you can get a little ahead.

**\*\*\***

The above article generated a lot of responses—pro and con—from many individuals. Some respondents also attempted to find "golden shooters" on whom they'd risk money after the shooter achieved the *5-Count*. Here are some examples of the letters (pro and con) I received concerning "The 24 Golden Shooters" article:

Dear Mr. Scoblete:
I took up your challenge and on a recent four-day trip to Atlantic City I decided to do exactly what you had done in Vegas [last] summer. Instead of one shooter per day, I bet only one shooter per casino on a single day. I walked from Showboat to Tropicana. I was too tired to make it to Hilton. As you did, I looked for a shooter who was setting the dice and taking careful aim with his rolls. I wound up betting on nine shooters for this experiment. I won on seven of them, lost on two of them. One shooter had a very good roll and made me some decent money.
Sincerely,
Robert B.
Philadelphia, PA

Dear Frank:

I hate to be the one to tell you that you are making a big mistake thinking that people can control the dice. But to be fair, I bet on six shooters who fit the description you gave in the article. Four of the shooters sevened out on the sixth or seventh roll. I lost on them. I won on two shooters. I don't doubt that you won on the 24 shooters but it just was an unusually good run of luck. It had nothing to do with the shooters controlling the dice.

However, I do realize that if you play as you suggest, the craps player will save himself a lot of money since he won't be getting into the action as much for the same amount of time at the table. So I do play the *5-Count* and I find that I am getting comped just as much for less risk. But I am not kidding myself as I think you are by thinking that some shooters can change the odds.

Still, I enjoy your books and your honesty when distinguishing between your "beliefs" and the "math" of the games.

Arnie W.
Los Angeles, CA

Dear Mr. Scoblete:

Puh-LEEZE! Controlling the dice? Rhythmic Rolling? The Captain? The *5-Count*! Next you'll be selling TARGET systems for blackjack. No one can control the dice and you are a moron if you think they can. I don't think you even bet on one shooter at craps, much less 24. I think you made up the article to fill space in your magazine and to push the worthless craps systems you sell in your books.

No, I have never played the so-called Captain's systems because I can tell in advance that they DON'T WORK. Get off it.

Michael D.
Dallas, TX

Dear Mr. Scoblete:

I, too, agree with The Sharpshooter's letter. . . . Two years ago I spent five days in St. Louis, Missouri with a young man whose name is "Bill." [editor's note: the letter contains real name of the person]. Presetting dice is his specialty and he is damned good at it. "Bill" has a lab near his residence. The lab is equipped with video cameras all around his dice table. He spends long hours pitching dice into a very small bowl. My conversations with "Bill" about presetting dice included the fact it takes a lot of practice. Also, it requires absolute body control and good depth of perception.

I cannot do what he does. I don't see many players capable of controlling dice via presetting for long periods either. But, I agree it's not only possible. I've seen it accomplished.

Marvin G.
South Bend, IN

Dear Mr. Scoblete:

I bet on 11 shooters in several days of play in Las Vegas a few weeks ago and I thought I'd write you a note to let you know I won on eight, lost on two, and broke even on one. I followed exactly what you described. I don't know if this means anything or not but I thought you'd like to know my results. I really enjoy *The New Chance and Circumstance* magazine. Keep up the good work.

Yours truly,
Amanda J.
Houston, TX

Dear Mr. Scoblete:

I spent a day in the casino but I would bet only those shooters who both made it past the *5-Count* and were fixing the dice and rolling in a controlled way. In six hours at various tables, I bet on 30 shooters. I won money on 19, lost on nine, and broke even on two. I made money. Yet, I spent most of the day just hanging around and watching which was not very satisfying. I think your Golden Shooter idea works but I don't think it is going to gain in popularity because you really don't have the fun associated with betting every shooter. For me, I'll continue to play the *5-Count* and take my chances with shooters who make it though the count but are not taking care with their rolls.

Mike M.
Los Angeles, CA

Dear "King" Scobe:

I played 17 "golden ones" on a recent trip to Atlantic City. Did it exactly as you suggested. Waited for the *5-Count* and only bet those players who had made it through the *5-Count* and were taking great care with their rolls. I won on 12 of them, lost on five of them. Not bad. One shooter had a pretty good roll and I was ahead a good deal because of that one shooter.

Carl L.
New York, NY

Dear Mr. Scoblete:

I undertook to do the same experiment as you. I found a total of 28 shooters in two days of searching for them and of them 13 won for me and 15 lost for me. But I came out ahead by a wide margin because the ones who had good rolls made me much more than what I lost on the ones I lost on. I think there is something to your idea.

Milton J.
Philadelphia, PA

Dear Frank:

I tried your Golden Shooter thing for 19 shooters on a recent trip to Vegas. I won on seven and I lost on 12. But I made money because one of the seven winners had a really good roll. Most of the tables I was watching were ice cold and the few good shooters came at long intervals. There may be something to what you're saying.

Tom C.
Phoenix, AZ

That article and hundreds of responses such as those, plus my experiences at the craps tables since then, have led me to formulate an advantage-play shooter-selection principle I have dubbed *The Golden Ruler*.

# The Golden Ruler

The Golden Ruler is how we measure which shooters we will risk money on at craps. The Golden Ruler must be applied with discipline and restraint. You are going to combine the *5-Count* with (potential) rhythmic rollers. It is a five-step process:

1. *Scout shooters.* When you see an individual who a.) sets the dice the same way each time, b.) uses a soft, controlled throw to the same area of the table each and every time, and c.) concentrates on what he is doing, you will bet on him after he passes the *5-Count*.

2. *Use the* 5-Count. The fact that someone is taking care with his roll is not a guarantee that he will have a good roll. He still must make it past the *5-Count* for you to risk money on him.

3. *Utilize low house-edge bets.* Keep the house edge 1.5 percent or under. That means the worst bets you'll make are the placing of the 6 and 8, the buying of the 4 and 10 in casinos that take the commission on winning bets only. The best bets you'll make are the Pass/Come with odds. Since you do not know what numbers another rhythmic roller's style might favor, you are better off making the lowest possible house edge bets based on the random game.

4. *When a shooter's rhythm changes, you change.* Be ready to call off your bets if a shooter changes his rhythm. That means you will actually adhere to one of the superstitions of craps—if a shooter's rhythm has been disrupted by another, or if the shooter doesn't set the dice the same way all of a sudden, or if the shooter takes too long of a pause after he gets the dice, or if he's bothered by the pit bringing out chip trays, or with the stickman fiddling with the dice, or if his spouse or significant other or friend starts to engage him in a conversation—"I'm off!" Keep those bets off until he settles back into his rhythm.

5. *Bet reasonable amounts.* Just because you are antsy to get into the action and you may have waited a long time to do so, doesn't

mean you should plunge in and bet more than normal. Just playing the *5-Count* for many players puts too much of a strain on their discipline, but utilizing the Golden Ruler will be much, much harder. You will find that you're anxious to put your money at risk.

You are going to be out of the action for prolonged periods of time if you play the Golden Ruler strictly. However, for those such as Mike M. from California, there is a way to get plenty of action at the tables and still apply the Golden Ruler technique. On those shooters who are not "golden," you will bet less money, and on those shooters who are "golden" you will bet more money.

## Betting Every Post *5-Count* Shooter

There are two broad categories of craps shooters: 1) rhythmic rollers, and 2) random rollers. Included in the rhythmic rolling category are those shooters who are conscious and unconscious (or temporary) rhythmic rollers. Of course, the overwhelming majority of shooters in the craps world are random rollers. The random rollers are your everyday craps players. Their rolls go something like this: The dealers pass them the dice, they pick the dice up and fling them down the table. Some of them don't even look to see where the dice land. Some look as if they don't care whether they win or lose and their rolls are desultory to say the least. Some might set the dice but then they shoot them so hard that the dice bing, bang and boom all over the place. These shooters are relying on luck for good rolls (and some will have good luck on some occasions) but in the end the casino will grind its edge out of their hides and from the hides of anyone who bets on them.

However, if you just don't have the patience to wait shooter after shooter for the "golden" ones who pop up somewhat infrequently, you can have you cake and eat it too. Here's how:

Let us say that you are a $225 player when you're up on three numbers. We'll assume a 2X Odds game (the most common in America). Let's say that you put $25 on the Pass Line or Come and back it with $50 in odds. When you're up on three numbers, you have $225 at risk. This is your normal method of playing. Simply, incorporating the *5-Count* into your playing scheme will radically reduce your overall risk because you will be eliminating between about one-half of all shooters you encounter. However, now you want to incorporate the Golden Ruler into your game plan as well. Let's see how to do that so that we radically reduce our overall risk.

*Scenario One:* Shooter A takes the dice and wings them down the table. It is evident that he is not attempting to be a rhythmic roller. But he makes it past the *5-Count*. When you would have normally put up your bets (on the 2-Count or 3-Count), instead of putting a $25 Pass or Come bet, you put a $10 Pass or Come bet and then, when the *5-Count* is achieved, back it with double odds. You go up on three numbers, just as you always do. You reduce your exposure from $225 to $90 or $100 (you'll put $25 in odds on the 6 and 8) on those shooters who are not taking care with their rolls. But you are still in the action.

*Scenario Two:* Shooter B gets the dice and you see that he is setting them a certain way, throwing them with care, and generally everything he does fits the profile of the rhythmic roller. For him, you will go back to your normal betting style.

The bottom line here is this: Bet much less on the random rollers and your usual betting level on the rhythmic rollers. In this way, you get the most money out on the shooters who have the very best chance to make you money but you still get to go up on all those shooters who make it past the *5-Count* despite the fact that they aren't in the rhythmic mode.

# SIX

# Step #4: Bet to Suit Your Purposes

The fourth principle for advantage-play craps is to utilize the best betting methods for your purposes. The standard of betting is always the Pass/Come with odds. This style reduces the house edge to its minimum when we are talking about a theoretical craps game where every roll is random. However, in the real world of craps play, where some shooters might be changing the odds, you might find that you will want to utilize other forms of betting. If you are playing to get comps, you might want to give the casino a slightly higher edge in order to get greater value in your comps—a value that transcends the casino's greater edge.

Since we don't know in advance which numbers most other rhythmic rollers will tend to throw, most times we will content ourselves with playing Pass/Come with odds or the *Supersystem*. However, if a shooter is having a good roll and is consistently hitting the 6 or 8, then placing those numbers in multiples of six dollars would not be an unwise decision. If the shooter is consistently hitting the 4 or 10 then buying these numbers in multiples of $25 (at casinos where the commission is only charged on winning bets) would also be a wise decision.

However, over time we should be able to figure out what numbers we tend to hit with a greater-than-probable frequency when we roll the dice. In my case, I tend to hit the 4, 6, 8 more often than normal and my greatest rolls have seen me hit the 6 and the Hard 6 an incredible number of times. In one case, I rolled nine straight Hardways—six of them the Hard 6, two the Hard 8, one the Hard 4. In another case, I rolled eight 6s in ten numbers. I do not seem to hit the 10 with any regularity and the 5 and 9 seems to have some good days and some bad days.

On my rolls in the last year, I have taken to going right up on the 6 and 8, sometimes without waiting for the *5-Count*, which is something I would never have considered even a few short years ago. Why am I doing this? Because I have been having excellent rolls where the 6 and 8 are repeating. Indeed, when it is my turn to roll, before I even get the dice, I'll say: "Sixty dollar 6 and 8." These numbers will, of course, be off on the Come Out roll. [As of this writing I am still debating whether my Hard 6 shooting warrants putting up a Hard 6 bet. This goes against my grain and I am not sure if my shooting can really overcome an almost double-digit house edge on the Hard 6. I may experiment with this, for very small amounts, and see how I do.]

There are two reasons for getting your Place bets up before your Come Out roll. The first concerns comps. Once those bets are up, the floorperson records them. You're getting credit for a bet that isn't at risk. On your Come Outs, if you should roll a bunch of 7s, you're making money on the Pass, getting comp points on your Place bets, and risking very little in the way of real cash. In the long haul, every roll you have that sees your money not at risk—but being recorded for comp purposes—is a favorable roll.

The second reason for getting your money up early in Place bets for your roll concerns the fact the more you have to fiddle with your betting while you're shooting, the greater the opportunity to screw up your rhythm. When you roll, the thing you want to focus on is your technique. By putting up Place bets, you can forget about the back and forth of the Come betting and just take down the profits as your numbers hit. Of course, I am not recommending Place betting over the traditional Pass/Come on such numbers as 5 or 9— unless you know without any doubts whatsoever that one, the other or both of these numbers are hit at extraordinary rates when you roll. Remember, even if you buy them for $38, the house still has a 2.56 percent edge for you to overcome. If you can't buy these numbers but must go with a traditional Place bet, the house edge of four percent is steep to say the least. However, if 6 and/or 8 are your numbers, Placing them on your roll might be a good idea.

But before you do any Place betting you must be reasonably assured that you have indeed perfected some kind of rhythmic roll. If you are not sure, then use the *5-Count* on yourself, just as you would any other player. Make the minimum Pass Line bet and then wait until you complete the *5-Count* before risking money on your own rolls. This is a judicious approach for those in doubt.

## How Much, How Many, How Long

How much should you bet? How many numbers should you cover? How long should you play for?

The Captain believes that gambling as a recreational activity falls into a class of activities known as "manageable thrills." He says: "It's a thrill ride that mixes an adrenaline rush with the opportunity to win money. It's excitement without any real danger if you literally and figuratively play your cards right." Therefore you don't want to bet so little that the results of a given roll are meaningless (would anyone reading this book really get a rush betting one penny on the Pass Line and backing it with two cents in odds?), and you don't want to bet so much that the results of a given roll could be you keeling over with a heart attack (could you see yourself betting your kid's college fund on the Pass Line and backing it with the mortgage in odds?).

Even as I postulate that my Golden Ruler method of play is an advantage-play craps technique I do so with the recreational gambler in mind—not with the "I want to make a living playing craps" player in mind—because the recreational gambler does not have to win to eat or pay the bills. If I am completely out of my mind and, in reality, mixing rhythmic rolling with *5-Counting* and low house-edge bets does not give the player an edge over craps, I still have done "no harm" to the recreational player. Such a player who follows the Golden Ruler, or one who plays the *5-Count* on all shooters, will be decreasing the total amount of money he is risking in the long haul, get more comps for less risk, and still get that adrenaline rush. This is a good thing. But if I am wrong and you have decided to use the Golden Ruler as a means of making a living at craps, then you could be in deep you-know-what and it's synonymous with the game.

I have always believed that a large bank to bet ratio makes for the best time at the tables for the recreational player. If you are going to bet $90 to $100 per roll when you are up on three numbers, then a session stake of $1,000 would be enough to play the Golden Ruler for a day and probably enough to sustain you for a session of several hours betting all shooters who make it past the *5-Count* using the method I explored in the last chapter—betting more on rhythmic rollers and betting less on random rollers. Therefore a total spread to bank ratio of 1:10 for a single session of play would be sufficient. That spread should be reflective of the high bet range, so if you are going up on three numbers for $100 for rhythmic rollers but only $50 on three numbers for all other post *5-Count* shooters, your stake would be $1,000 for a session.

How much should you have in your total bankroll given the above example? You should have enough to last at least 10 sessions, if not twice that number. Even with $20,000 backing your $100 at risk—when your money is riding on those cubes, the thrill will be there, but it won't be enough to kill you should you lose.

How many numbers should you cover? That's up to you. The more numbers, the more often you will be involved in decisions, the fewer the numbers, the less often your numbers will be decided. If you want to bet $90 are you better off betting it all on one number or on three numbers? The math says it doesn't matter in the long run. If you are betting $30 on the Pass with $60 in odds, the casino will have the same long-term edge on you as when you bet $10 on the Pass with $20 in odds along with two Come numbers of the same amounts. The difference will be in the pattern of your wins and loss-es, not the general long-run outcome. That's the math. As a rhythmic roller, if you know that you hit the 6 on a greater-than-probable fre-quency and that all the other numbers are subpar—then you would want to put your whole amount on the 6. This is an area where "know thyself" is the key philosophical and tactical dictum.

How long should you play for? Again this is a very subjective area and I have gone into great detail in many of my other books con-cerning how to decide when to call it a session. Suffice it to say that with the Golden Ruler technique, you will probably spend much more time searching for shooters than actually betting on shooters and correspondingly you will probably spend more time in the casino on any given trip than someone who is playing the "bet all" post *5-Count* shooters. Even if you are playing with an edge by using the Golden Ruler technique, you would still be wise to maintain your own rhythm and not press the action. A combination of time spent, money won or lost, and fatigue will determine when to call it a session or a day. Veteran casino players seem to know intuitively when the time is right for taking a break. If you're getting blasted out early—shooter after shooter sevening out just after making the *5-Count*—that might be a signal to take some time off to catch your breath. You do not have to lose an entire session stake to finish a negative session. Money you save in one session is money that can be used in the future. As with life, love, and the pursuit of gambling riches, you can't force Lady Luck to give you her favors each and every time you play. If she isn't smiling on you, she isn't smiling on you. A nice break is often what you need to clear your head and ready yourself for your next battle with the casino.

# SEVEN

# Step #5: Winning the Comp Game

Thus far in this book I've discussed a very straightforward attack against the casinos at the craps table that consists of making low house-edge bets, developing your rhythmic rolling style, playing the *5-Count* and utilizing the Golden Ruler for shooter selection in order to reduce risk and enhance your opportunity to be on the hot shooters—and enhance the possibility that often *you will be that hot shooter*. In short, the first four steps show you how to beat *the game* of craps as it is played in the real world of casinos.

But there is another game that is played in casinos as well. It is played at every table and on every machine and it is played every minute of every day. The casino is well aware of this second game; in fact, the casino is expert at playing this second game, while most players just bumble along never thinking that this second game can be exploited for the player's benefit. This second game is the comp game.

Most casino players are cognizant that their action in a casino can be monitored by the floorperson (or, for slot players, the computers in the machines) and that the casino is willing to give a certain percentage of a player's action back to him in the form of comps (short for complimentaries).

Now, as long as you have a player's card and hand it in at the beginning of your session, you will get whatever comps the casino feels you deserve. If you're a big bettor, you'll get the deluxe treatment known as RFB—room, food, beverage with exclusive parties, shows, and gifts including cash back and match play coupons; medium players will get RLF—room, limited food with discounted shows, some gifts, and cashback/coupons; lower level players will get discounted rooms, discounted food and an occasional premium in the form of cashback, matchplay, or gifts.

There is no absolute rule as to what betting levels constitute what levels of comps. It depends on the individual casino. Treasure Island on the Strip in Las Vegas might give RFB to a $170 craps player ($60 on the 6 and 8, with a $50 buy of the 4 or 10) who plays for four hours; while The Four Queens in Downtown Las Vegas might require half that much for the top comps. Some casinos will take into account your full spread in figuring comps, others will not include the odds. Thus, if you go up on three numbers with $25 on the Pass/Come and $50 in odds on each, you get rated as a $75 player not as a $225 player. Indeed, *most* casinos do not include the odds in calculating comps since the odds bet is a break-even proposition.

To successfully maneuver in the minefield of the comp wars, you first have to know what your action is worth to the casino where you want to play. If you decide to take a trip to a new casino, call the casino in advance and ask to speak to a shift manager or a host. Explain how you intend to bet and probe for the formula that they will use to rate your play. You can do this straightforwardly: "I want full RFB and I'll be playing craps. What do I have to bet and how long do I have to bet it for?"

If the host or shift manager says: "You have to bet $150 for four hours," don't settle for that. Ask how that $150 can be spread out. Will odds count in the figuring? If not, is $60 on the 6 and 8, with a $30 buy of the 4 or 10 considered a $150 bet? You want to get them to commit to concrete figures. Most casinos will be more than happy to share with you the exact types of betting that they're looking for (actually, they'd love for you to make the Crazy Crapper bets). If the casino host or the shift manager is reluctant to talk to you or blows you off by making it sound as if their formula for rating you is a top secret, then blow them off and take your action elsewhere.

The second way to approach a casino is to explain how you intend to bet and ask what you'll get in return.

"I will be placing line bets of $10 each and putting odds behind them of $20. I'll be up on three numbers when I'm done. What is that action worth in comps? Do you count the odds in your figures? Am I a $30 player or a $90 player? How long do I have to play this way to get a free room? How long do I have to play to get a comp to the cafe?"

If you bet a combination of Pass Line with Place betting (for those of you who are rhythmic rollers), make sure you know exactly what each bet gets you.

That's the first step. Ask questions and know exactly what your action is worth.

The second step is really very simple. Very simple indeed. Regardless of how you are betting, you will utilize the *5-Count*. This will reduce by 50 percent (sometimes more), the number of shooters you are risking your money on. If you have to play four hours a day to get the full range of comps that you desire, playing the *5-Count* will reduce the total risk time to approximately two hours, even though your body will be at the tables for the requisite four hours.

How can this help you in the comp game? Watch.

If we take an average bet of $100 at craps, the typical casino will postulate that the player is going to lose between 1.5 and 3.5 percent of his total action. The casino might figure approximately 60 decisions for that $100 bettor, thus the "expected theoretical loss" is between $90 and $180 for one hour of play. The expected loss for full comping purposes will be between $360 and $720 for four hours of play. Most casinos are willing to give back between 30 and 50 percent of the theoretical loss in the form of comps. That means the cheap casinos (30 percent) will give back between $108 and $216; and generous casinos will be giving back between $180 and $360. While that is some range in *compspectation* between casinos, the fact remains that a wide range of returns exists in the real world of play.

Let us assume that the casino where you play is neither cheap (30 percent) nor generous (50 percent) but average (40 percent). Let us further speculate that it uses 2.5 percent as its theoretical house edge at craps (many use this very figure). If you are betting $100 for four hours at 60 decisions per hour, you are putting into action

$24,000 into action with an expected loss of $600. The casino will return $240 in the form of comps to you. This would probably mean a free room (or a heavily discounted room) and free meals at the cafe.

By utilizing the *5-Count*, you are cutting the number of decisions by approximately 50 percent. Nor are you making high house-edge bets. In fact, if you are Placing the 6 and 8, you're facing a house edge of around 1.52 percent, not the theoretical 2.5 percent that is being used for comps. Instead of an expected loss of $600, your expected loss is only $365 for four hours of action. Ah, but you aren't giving the casino four *real* hours of action, you are only giving 50 percent of that. Your real-world "expected loss" will be approximately $183 and your comps will be $240! That $57 difference is a *monetary* advantage!

Naturally, if the casino counts the odds portion of your Pass Line and Come bets as a part of your rating criteria, you can get an overwhelming monetary edge as your expected losses will be minuscule compared to the comp returns you can expect to get.

Of course, the monetary edge puts money indirectly in your pocket by allowing you to get free or discounted rooms, food and whatever else the casino is offering. Still, once a trip to your favorite casino is over, you can't cash out whatever value in comps you didn't use. If you were entitled to free show tickets and you didn't go to the show, you can't ask for the value of those show tickets in cash. I wish you could! However, it is still better to have a monetary edge than to not have it.

Combined with *5-Counting* and even a modified form of the Golden Ruler (bet more on those players who seem to be rhythmic rollers, less on those players who get past the *5-Count* but are random rollers), a recreational player has a tremendous shot to be a long-term winner at craps. There is no better feeling than to get more comps than your action is really worth and simultaneously be winning money at the tables as well!

## Scobe's Tricks for Comp Treats

The *5-Count* will reduce your overall exposure but there are additional things to do that can help you get a good comp rating—things that won't cost you a penny more than you intended to bet.

1. *Get rated when not at risk.* When a person has reached the 4-Count and will be on the Come Out roll for the *5-Count*, put up your Pass Line bet and all your Place bets at this time. The Place bets will be recorded by the rater but will be off (not working), while your Pass Line bet is a two to one favorite during the fifth roll.

2. *Tip on the top.* When you are tipping, put the tip *on top of your bet*, not next to it. If your normal way of tipping is to make a Pass Line bet for the dealers, you are getting no comp credits for that bet if it is next to your own Pass Line bet. Instead, put it on top. Thus, if you are a $25 Pass Line bettor and want to bet five dollars for the dealers, just put it on top and tell the dealers: "The red chip on top is for the dealers." You'll make the dealers happy and the rater will include that five dollars in your rating. What's more, if you do win the bet, the dealers will only win the five dollars of the win; they will not have to take down their share of the Pass Line bet (the usual procedure) as that belongs to you. Had the tip been next to your bet, they would have taken it along with the win. By tipping on top, you get to keep the tip in play roll after roll, getting comp credit after comp credit, without any more than the initial risk.

If you like to make Hardways bets for the dealer, you must not let them have control of the bet. If you would normally make a five-dollar bet for them on a Hardway number, throw it up but say: "I win this—I'm going to share it with the dealers." Do *not* say, "two-way Hardway" because then the boxman will want to split the bet up and you'll only get credit for that portion of the Hardway that is for you. (You shouldn't be betting Hardways unless you are rolling rhythmically and you know that you make this or that Hardway often enough to overcome a monumental house edge! Otherwise tip on top of your Pass Line bet to get the comp credit.)

3. *Be ready to call off your bets.* Call off your bets if the shooter isn't hitting your numbers according to this formula:

a. If you are on three numbers and the shooter hasn't hit one of them in four consecutive rolls, call your bets off for two rolls. On the second of the two rolls, if the shooter hits any one of the point numbers, let your bets work again. If on the second of the two rolls, he hits a garbage number (2, 3, 11, or 12), wait until he rolls a point number before going back up. Why do this? We're looking for shooters who are repeating point numbers, not garbage. If the shooter is in a garbage rhythm, it is possible that the ultimate garbage number, the 7, is itching to rear its ugly head.

b. If you are on four numbers or five numbers, call your bets off if after three consecutive rolls fails to hit one of them. Use the above formula for determining when to start your bets working again.

c. If you are on all six numbers, call your bets off if two consecutive rolls fail to hit one of them.

d. If a rhythmic roller changes his style for the various reasons mentioned in the previous chapter.

When you call your bets off, you are not "taking down" the bet. You do not want the Place bets returned, you do not want the odds removed. You're just off for a couple of rolls. Tell the dealers to put the "off" button on your bets if they are confused. "Off button my bets." You will lose no comp points when you temporarily call off bets. In fact, your rating will continue—with no risk to your money!

4. *Time your entry to maximize your first impression.* Try to enter a game on a shooter who has just made or is about ready to make the 5-Count. It is sometimes a little awkward to cash in and then wait two or three consecutive shooters before putting your money at risk (which will often happen). Raters are looking for that first bet to put down their first impression of your action. Indeed, if you can, try to make your entrance on a Golden Shooter—that is, one taking extreme care with his technique—and then get your biggest bet recorded as your first impression!

5. *Enter the game when you are about to shoot.* If you are an accomplished rhythmic roller, then enter a game when you are about to shoot. That just means that if the dice are coming to the spot you like and that spot is open, go for it! In this way, you go up immediately and get those big bets recorded.

6. *Comp as you go.* Get your comps up front and don't wait until the end of your stay to settle up. Many hosts will tell you to "charge it to your room" and at the end of your trip they'll pick up whatever your play warrants. My experience has been that it is better to get your comps up front—comp as you go—rather than wait for the end. This advice was brought home to me recently at one Vegas casino that is noted for being very tight with comps. I was waiting to see the host to assess what I would get for my projected play and one other man was ahead of me. Here's the conversation:

Host: "We have you down as a $100 blackjack player playing for 12.5 hours for three days. We'll pick up your room and $300 in food for your stay."

Player: "Wait a minute, didn't you say at this level of betting I was RLF [room, limited food] and that I could charge everything from the non-gourmet rooms and you'd pick it up?"

Host: "Our policy is to pick up the non-gourmet up to a certain point. You charged approximately $180 per day to your room in food bills. . ."

Player: "My wife eats a lot."

Host: "About $498 worth of food and we'll pick up $300 worth."

Player: "But I lost $2,375!"

Host: "Whether you win or lose isn't the issue, how much you bet, for how long, is how we decide what to give you."

I then decided to try a little experiment. I would mimic this player's betting level and hours played, but I would ask for my comps up front for everything but the gourmet rooms. Those I would charge to my room. My breakfasts, (total cost $20), and my lunches (approximately $40) were comp as you go. I stayed three days and got comps for $180 up front. (When I asked for a comp, pit bosses inquired if I was staying at the hotel. I answered yes but I prefer to get comps this way. No one turned me down.) I charged $487 in gourmet meals to my room. At the end of my three days I went to the host.

Host: "We have you listed as playing 12.5 hours at $100 per hand. We'll pick up your room and $300 of your food."

Me: "Thank you, that's very generous of you."

In fact, by getting my non-gourmet comps up front I was given $480 in comps for food, while the player I mimicked had only received $300 for food. Whether this stratagem will work at every casino is hard to say but you can't lose anything by trying it. So get those comps up front!

8. *High rollers should get RFB upfront.* If you are a high roller according to a casino's formula, then make it a point to establish that all your comps are upfront. Nothing should be left to the discretion of a pit boss, host, or casino manager. If they told you that your level of play merits a free room, limo service, show tickets, free gourmet, the exclusive party, massages, and whatnots . . . then there should never be a question at the end of your stay as to what you're getting. I've heard some variation of this argument a dozen times:

Patron: "There's a charge on my room for the spa?"

Host: "Yes, sir, we don't cover the spa on your comps."

Patron: "But I was told I'd get everything."

Host: "Everything but the spa, sir."

Patron: "I thought everything meant everything?"

Host: "It does, except for the spa, sir."

The best answer the patron can make to this insistence that *everything doesn't mean everything* is to whip out a letter from the "boss" (whoever that boss happens to be: the head host, the shift manager, the casino manager, the CEO) and show it to the host.

Patron: "See, here, when I called and said I was coming I asked for a letter telling me what I could get for my action. This here letter says that everything will be comped. It didn't say the spa wouldn't be. In fact, note this line here: 'And your wife will have full spa privileges.' What does that mean to you?"

Host: "We comp everything including the spa!"

Patron: "Thank you, I enjoyed my stay."

Host: "Great, come back again real soon."

8. *Delay your exit from the game.* If you know that you are finished with a session, don't leave right away. Instead, take a bathroom break and tell them to save your spot. While you're at the bathroom, your comp rating continues. When you get back to the table color up. "Just realized I was late for dinner!"

9. *Don't be a pig.* When a casino comps you for a gourmet dinner, especially if there isn't a cap on the meal [a "cap" is a monetary limit on what the casino will pay], don't eat more than you'd normally eat or order drinks/wines you wouldn't normally order. You may think that you're pulling a fast one on the casino by "soaking them for all they're worth" but in reality such piggish behavior damages you in two ways. The first concerns close calls on your next trip. If you are in the high-roller–by–a–nose category, you might find that the casino host is reluctant to give you unlimited RFB next time because the last time you ate and drank and ran up a tab as if there were no tomorrow. But there was a tomorrow and that becomes today when the Host tells you: "Sorry, Mr. Horta, but your meal is now capped at $150 for you and your lovely sow." The second kind of damage is merely moral in nature: Do you want to be thought of as swine? Do you want to be viewed as someone who is an ungracious guest? Someone who takes advantage of a casino's hospitality? Consider

this as well: Many casinos have tightened their gourmet comping policies because of the gluttonous behavior of some high rollers. Thus, players who might have just eked out a gourmet comp, now are rejected.

But lack of class is not just the province of a few high rollers. Awful behavior in comped situations extends up and down the comp scale. Here's an example of swinish behavior from a group of comped low-rollers that I personally witnessed at Treasure Island in Las Vegas.

Ten people had buffet comps. The restaurant set up a long table and these Neanderthals proceeded to do the following: they each took several plates and loaded them with everything that was being served. They then took several more plates and brought seconds back to the table before they finished—before they *touched*—their firsts. They then ate as much as they could from plate to plate—a little of this, a little of that, some of these. Each person ordered several drinks—sodas, juices, water—but only drank sips from one or the other before ordering a different beverage. The table got so crowded with dishes and glasses (not one of which was ever completely free of food or empty of drink so that the waitresses could not clear part of the table to make room) that small tables were placed on either end of the long table to accommodate the overflow. When these "patrons" were finished with their main meal, they headed for the dessert area where each one took three or four different desserts. These they placed on the table. Then each one headed back to the dessert area and made him or herself a huge overflowing sundae. They placed the sundaes by their other desserts and. . . .

*Then they left!*

I stood up and saw them in the casino. They were laughing and slapping "high fives" with each other for the remarkable "joke" they had played on . . . whom? The casino owner? The pit boss who gave them the comp? The gods of chance? The poor servers who had to watch their nastiness? "Oh, yeah, baby! Oh, baby, slap me five! Ha! Ha! Ha! Ha!"

The sundaes began to melt as the concerned waitresses looked at each other as if to say: "Are they coming back? What should we do?"

I was an interested witness to this bizarre event. After 15 minutes, with sundaes dripping onto untouched salads and half-eaten sausages, someone must have given the signal to clear the table. All that food, all those desserts, all that effort expended by the servers on a herd of swine.

And the bastards didn't even leave a tip.

So when you're comped, just behave normally. Eat what you would normally eat, drink what you would normally drink. Enjoy the meal for the meal it is, not for the fact that you were able to make the buttons of your pants or blouse explode. While I want you to take the casinos for all they are worth, I want you to do it in a worthwhile and classy way.

So be a gourmet—not a gourmand.

# The Full-Blown Attack

Let's recap before moving on. The full-blown attack on the casino coffers can yield a positive monetary and, perhaps, mathematical result if you incorporate as many of the following into your playing arsenal as possible:

1. *Learn to be a rhythmic roller.* So take care with your rolls and develop your style.

2. *Use the* 5-Count. Never bet a shooter who hasn't yet made it through. The only exception is if you (or someone you know) is a demonstrated rhythmic roller. I now go up on myself immediately.

3. *Utilize the Golden Ruler* either fully or partially by betting more on rhythmic rollers and less on random rollers.

4. *Make the best bets to suit your purposes.* More often than not these bets will be the lowest house-edge bets, but at times you might want to place certain numbers if these are the numbers that you tend to hit more often than probability indicates.

5. *Maximize comps* whenever possible.

# EIGHT

# The Anatomy of an Epic Roll

T he greatest craps roll of my life—April 2, 1999—came at the right time and place. It had a context over and above the money people made while it happened. It wasn't just an epic craps roll; it was a saving of face, a vindication, a miracle wrought by a divine hand! At least, that's what it seemed to me at the time and even now as I reflect upon it.

*Chicago Sun Times* columnist and author John Grochowski and I were guest authors at The Meet the Authors Easter weekend at the Golden Nugget. At an afternoon seminar on Friday, April 2 were Barry Dickerson and his son Pete. Also Bill Burton, editor of the About.com gambling webpage, and John Robison, managing editor of my website (www.scoblete.com) on the RGT Online pages and columnist for *Chance and Circumstance* and other magazines.

*BARRY DICKERSON: I've read all Frank's books on craps. I wanted to see Frank play craps and use the 5-Count. I have listened to Frank's craps tape many times. I wanted to meet him and the beautiful A.P. I wanted to see Frank "Roll Them Bones."*

"I want to play craps with you and see you have one of your good rolls. Can we do that?" said Barry.

"Sure, no problem. After dinner," I said.

After the seminar, in the elevator, I turned to my wife, the beautiful A.P., and said: "I'm dead."

"What?"

"I'm dead," I said. "Dead. Barry *drove* all the way from Tennessee to see me have one of my good rolls."

In our room, A.P. said: "You've been having good rolls for two years."

"And tonight all you're going to hear is seven-out! seven-out! seven-out! within seconds every time I get the dice."

"If that happens everyone will understand," said A.P. calmly.

"He quoted me," I whispered.

"What?"

"Barry quoted whole sections of my tape from memory," I said.

"He must like it," said A.P.

"I'm dead."

*BILL BURTON: Barry, Pete and I started the evening as Frank's dinner guests at Stefano's along with the Beautiful A.P., John and Marcy Grochowski, John Robison and Rick Barton, whose travel agency, Make Your Bet, was sponsoring the weekend. During dinner we discussed the Captain's 5-Count and the philosophy of rhythmic rolling. Frank has written extensively about shooters controlling the dice. He attributes his good rolls to setting the dice.*

After dessert, the moment of truth arrived.

"Well," said Bill Burton, "Are we playing craps?"

The consensus was that we should head across the street to Binions since it had 10X odds. On the way there, I visualized the dice being passed to me by the stickman, my setting them with the three-spots in an inverted "V" and then lofting them gently so that they'd hit the back wall on one bounce without rebounding all over the layout. I believe this method of shooting has helped me to have many good rolls the past two years.

Is it possible for a person to control the dice enough to turn a slightly negative game into a slightly positive game? Opinion is split. All other gaming authorities say no—I say yes. In point of fact, and tongue now out of my cheek, most gaming authorities routinely dismiss the idea that shooters can physically control the dice. Orthodox craps thinking postulates that since the dice have to hit the back wall, a craps shoot is strictly random. I once believed that orthodoxy. But over the years I've witnessed too many good rolls by "The Arm" in Atlantic City and I've had enough good rolls myself that now I tend to believe rhythmic rolling is real. Real enough to change the odds slightly in the player's favor by reducing the appearance of the seven and/or increasing the appearance of point numbers. Of course, these rhythmic rollers are in a distinct minority and to find them requires a screening method—how do you decide which shooters to take a gamble on? I use the Captain's *5-Count*.

*BARRY DICKERSON: At dinner Frank urged all of us to use the 5-Count when playing at the same table with him—even when he rolled. When we rolled he told us just to make the minimum Pass Line bet, don't back it with odds, until the 5-Count was completed.*

Friday night, April 2, and Binions was crowded. If you've never been to Binions in Vegas it is an aural and olfactory experience—decades of cigarettes and cigars mixed liberally with dashed hopes and dreams catalyzed by the adrenaline rush of outrageous fortune. If there are gaming ghosts haunting any Vegas casino—they rattle their chains at the Horseshoe. John Grochowski decided to play video poker so he wandered off into the smoky fog of a slot aisle. Marcy, A.P. and John Robison stood at the bar which was right near the table where we would be playing. A.P. gave me a thumbs up sign as we settled in.

*BILL BURTON: Frank took the position to the stickman's right. Barry was at the stickman's left. I stood at the corner on Frank's right, allowing enough room between us to let us shoot comfortably while giving me a clear view to observe his shooting style. Pete took his place to my right. I had made a decision that tonight I would use the 5-Count exactly as Frank advocates. The first shooter failed to make the 5-Count. Pete got the dice and had the same results. It was my turn to shoot. Years ago, the first book I read was Frank's* Beat the Craps Out of the Casinos. *Now, here I was at the craps table with him. I set the dice with the fives up. I found that this worked better for me than the threes up that Frank uses. I placed my Pass Line bet and let the dice fly. "Seven! Pay the line!" the stickman called. "All Right!" I thought. My euphoria was short lived. I threw again and, after establishing my point, I sevened out.*

When it came time for me to shoot, I placed a minimum Pass Line bet (the table minimum was $5). The stickman passed me the dice and I selected two. I set the dice in the "V" formation. I didn't feel quite right, my jacket was pulling on me. I established my point, then rolled another number, and then on the 3-Count I sevened out. I noticed that Rick had placed odds behind his Pass Line bet and had been up on the second number with odds as well. Rick had also gone up on the three previous shooters. He had taken a pretty bad hit— four shooters in a row sevening out before the *5-Count*.

Then Barry, Rick and the two others sevened out early, although Barry and Rick had made it past the *5-Count*. I lost money on those rolls. Then the man next to Pete rolled and he sevened out early as well. Then Pete sevened out fast, too. At that point, Rick left the table. He had bet on every shooter and had lost his session stake in a little more than one circuit of the table. Bill whispered something to the effect: "Thank God for the *5-Count*" just before it was his turn to roll.

Unfortunately, Bill also sevened out quickly and now it was my turn again. As everyone had been rolling, I had been studying my "spot" on the back wall. I always try to hit the area of the back wall just a fraction before it starts to curve towards the stickman. I was memorizing the spot and trying to get a feel for it. I took off my jacket and handed it to A.P.

A dealer snickered: "He means business." The other dealers' eyes rolled. How many times had they seen shooters get ready for great rolls and then . . . seven-out!

"God," I prayed as the stickman passed me the dice, "Please don't let me embarrass myself."

I set the dice in the "V" and aimed for my spot.

And then it began. My first point, I recall, was 5. I rolled a few numbers, passed the *5-Count*, placed my odds, rolled some numbers as I was placing Come bets and taking odds, then: "Five! Five! Winner five!"

*BARRY DICKERSON: I saw how intense Scobe was when he rolled. How he concentrated. He would just stare at the dice and stare down the table. He rolled the same way each and every time. He was like a machine.*

I felt comfortable. I felt that when I established a second point, if I could roll a few numbers before it, then hit the second point, I would have acquitted myself well. On the next Come Out roll I placed a Hard 6 for the dealers. Once at Binions, I had a remarkable roll that consisted of nine hardways in succession, six of them the Hard 6.

Again my point was 5. I rolled a few numbers and then: "Five! Five! Winner five!" Okay, I thought to myself, you've been hitting numbers—no garbage.

It was my third Come Out roll. My mind was focused. I could clearly see my spot on the back wall. I thought: "I'm happy the dealers are returning the dice so quickly."

Now, the dream began.

The next point was also a 5. I rolled some numbers, then hit it again. I had been playing three numbers with full odds and I decided on the next point to go up on the Come and eventually get on all the numbers—although I would not take full odds but reduce the odds so I wasn't risking much more on six numbers than I had on three numbers. I made this decision—in some corner of my mind—when I had rolled three nines in a row.

I don't remember what my next point was—in fact, from this moment I have only a dreamy awareness of the multitude of numbers I rolled, but I remember it was during the pursuit for this point that a classic pattern began.

*BILL BURTON: After he established his next point the numbers started to come one after another. Suddenly a guy came up and asked me how the table was. I told him it had been cold, hoping he wouldn't try to squeeze in. No luck. He pushed his way in between Frank and me, bumping Frank as he did, and almost burning me with his cigarette. "Oh, no!" I thought when he bumped Frank, "He is going to break his rhythm."*

The rudest kind of behavior at a craps table is to push your way in next to a shooter who is having a good roll. It is especially rude to physically touch the shooter. Well, this guy not only pushed me, he started to talk to me, and blew smoke in my face. I turned from him, ignored him, but I could feel that I was not in the dreamlike state any more. I called my odds off. Then I tried to concentrate. Look at your spot, I said to myself, set the dice, get your rhythm back.

*A.P.: At this point, Scobe had been rolling for about 15 minutes or so. I was watching out of the corner of my eye. Then Rick came back from watching the light show and said: "He's still rolling?" Marcy had gone to talk to her husband but when she came back she said: "Is he still rolling?"*

*BILL BURTON: I saw him tell the dealers to take his odds bets off. At this point I held my breath. I had visions of the seven. The next few rolls were garbage but then he seemed to get back in the groove with a few numbers. He told the dealers to start his odds working again and he immediately made his point. The players cheered.*

I was in an altered state of consciousness. It was me, the dice, my spot and nothing else. I couldn't tell you if people were cheering when numbers were rolled or the points were hit. To me the world was silent. When the roll was over I asked A.P. if anyone cheered while it was going on and she said that they had. I didn't hear them. I can liken my consciousness to a movie where the camera makes everything fuzzy except a single object. For me, the dice and my spot were crystal clear, the world at large was fuzzy. But I do recall that my numbers came in bunches—two or three fours, then tens in a row, then I'd hit my point, then several sixes, a few eights, bam, bam, back to back, 9, 9, 9, 6, 6, 10, 10, 10, "Five! Winner Five!" Again I was cognizant that the dealers were getting me the dice quickly, in fact they were getting them to me with the three-spots showing!

*MARCY GROCHOWSKI: I had never witnessed a good roll like this and I wanted to walk over to see how much money everyone was making. But when I started to move to the table A.P. grabbed my arm and told me not to. "If he sees you, even out of the corner of his eye, you know what will happen." So I stayed put. But the looks on the faces of the people at that table were something to see even though I couldn't see exactly how much money everyone was making.*

*RICK BARTON: I could see the racks filling up with chips, then the colors of the chips changing to higher denominations—it was like a beautiful butterfly. Had I played the 5-Count I would have been at the table when Frank had his roll. It was a lesson to me in patience. Gambling lessons come hard!*

*A.P.: Somewhere in the middle of the roll, maybe the 25 minute mark, I commented to John Robison, "I wonder when they're going to bring the chip trays over to interrupt his rhythm?"*

*BILL BURTON: There were plenty of chips and a refill wasn't necessary. They came with a couple of racks and dropped them down in the middle of the layout as Frank was shooting, trying to break his rhythm. Frank has written about this in his books, but this was the first time I had actual-*

*ly witnessed it in person. This must not have bothered Frank. He kept rolling numbers and finally made his point yet again.*

I noticed the chip trays but I also noticed that the dealers pushed them over to the boxman. I was betting for the dealers as were most of the other players at the table. They were making money and didn't want to see the roll end either. The only glance I got at the pit boss—a bald, red-faced man—showed him to be frowning and concerned. But in my dreamlike state, he seemed far, far away, in some other dimension.

I continued to roll. I had no idea for how long. I also have no idea how many points I made or how many numbers I rolled. I do know that at times I felt a giddiness well up inside me—I wanted to laugh! I was joyous in one part of my being, steady and workmanlike in another part. Even as I rolled I had a split consciousness, a part of me was watching another part of me roll them bones.

I sevened out when one die glanced a chip and rolled on the 1 instead of the 2—the other die was a 6.

There was a pause . . . then I clapped. I don't recall if anyone else clapped. I wasn't clapping for myself. I was clapping in thanks for answered prayers. It then hit me that I just had a phenomenal roll, the best of my life—maybe six garbage numbers the whole time, mostly when that guy pushed me. I had been in a zone, a rolling zone, and the subjective experience felt as if there was nothing random about it. I looked down at my chip rack—all four rows were filled to capacity.

I turned to find A.P. I didn't know if she had been watching. Then I saw her and she was clapping—then I realized that Rick and John Robison and Marcy were also clapping. I was out of the dream and into reality. I could hear the background noise of the casino.

After we cashed in our stacks of chips at the cage, Barry came over to me. "I just gotta give you a big hug. I am in hog heaven!" And he hugged me. Pete shook my hand! Bill Burton bowed and said: "I believe! I believe!" Rick slapped my back: "I witnessed a once-in-a-lifetime event!"

On the way back to the Golden Nugget I asked John Robison how long the roll lasted. "A minimum of 45 minutes, maybe closer to an hour," he replied.

"All numbers, too," I said to no one in particular.

*BILL BURTON: As we walked across the street to the Golden Nugget, I thought "David has slain Goliath."*

*A.P.: Luck is timing and Scobe had timed his greatest roll perfectly. Tonight, in front of so many witnesses, he had come through like no one could come through. And everything happened at that craps table exactly as he has written about it over the years—the guy jostling in, the casino bringing in the chip trays, the efficacy of the 5-Count and an epic roll to boot! Everything happened as if Scobe had written it for a movie script.*

The next night, at the big Golden Nugget reception, a young lady said to me: "Everyone's talking about your great roll last night. My husband and I want you to roll for us tonight."

"I'm never playing craps again!" I laughed.

*JOHN ROBISON: The news spread through downtown Las Vegas faster than food poisoning at a 99-cent buffet. The buzz along Fremont Street was: "Where were you when Frank Scoblete had his monster roll at Binion's?" Whenever something exciting happens somewhere, I'm usually at the point farthest from it. But this time I had a front row seat! Here's what I saw: Frank rolled and rolled and rolled and rolled.*

# NINE

# The Best Strategies for the Dark Side of Craps

More than 90 percent of craps players are *Right* or *Do* bettors. This means that they bet with the dice or shooter and against the 7. They want that shooter to establish a point, make that point, and continue this process until the Judgment of the Dead or until the casino runs out of money, whichever comes first. (Probably the Judgment of the Dead!) In fact, craps is so dominated by *Do* bettors that most of the literature, language and lore of the game come from this side of the table. Tales of epic rolls, great shooters, charismatic players fill many a craps book, including this one, and many a craps player's imagination.

The overwhelming majority of the mail that I get regarding craps deals with the right side of the game. Rarely do I receive mail from someone interested in . . . the *other* side.

But there is another side to craps, a side that is frowned upon by the majority of the craps-playing public, a side traditionally known as *Wrong* or *Don't*, but today most commonly referred to as *The Dark Side* in honor of that epic villain Darth Vader of *Star Wars* fame. For players who have given themselves over to the Dark Side of craps, the side that roots for the 7 and against the shooter, there are no magnificent tales of epic rolls or wonderful shooters, because Darksiders don't desire epic rolls. They want quick calls of "seven-out, pay the don't!" They desire cold tables. They desire bad rolls. They desire lousy shooters. But all their desires they must desire quietly. You'll rarely hear Darksiders shouting for the seven to appear because that would offend the orthodoxy of the Do players, an orthodoxy that is often loud, as often truculent, and always peevish when it comes to the blasphemers betting the *wrong* way. The Darksider's relationship to the Right side is similar to a witch's relationship to the medieval church. Best not to draw too much attention to yourself or you might find yourself in a hot and uncomfortable situation.

So, often you will see Darksiders skulking about craps tables and surreptitiously placing their Don't Pass and Don't Come bets. If they win, they collect their chips quickly-quietly and quickly-quietly deposit them in their racks. Rarely do they make eye contact with a Right player because to do so is tantamount to making eye contact with a pit bull. Occasionally, when you hear them say such things as: "Fifty dollars no four!" or "Lay against the ten!" whole tables have been known to turn as one and glare at the man (or rarely, the woman) so doing. The good earth rumbles with discontent when the Darksider makes himself known. And right bettors wish the ground could open up and swallow them. I know. I've seen it with my own eyes.

I was in Atlantic City a while back, doing interviews and, when I had some free moments, playing with the Captain and some of his Crew. Two Darksiders arrived at our table, which had been cold for about 30 minutes. Luckily, by utilizing the Captain's *5-Count*, I had not lost much money in that time and my hopes of a good roll bailing me out were still high. I was in a good mood. However, other Right bettors at the table had taken a bath, a beating, a blasting—you get the alliterative picture—and they were in bad, bad, bad moods. That's when the two Darksiders appeared.

"Scum," whispered the man to my right, a cantankerous old craps player from World War II. He indicated the Darksiders, "They shouldn't allow them to play. They bring bad luck."

Another man, somewhat younger but with markedly fewer teeth, spit out: "There's no room at the table!" He then moved to take up two positions. "There's plenty of room," stated the boxman whose job it is to make sure as many people can squeeze onto a table as possible. "Here, right here." The Boxman indicated me. "Right next to this guy."

The Darksiders looked at me. I looked at them. They moved to either side of me. The old World War II guy picked up his chips and left in an harrumph.

It so happened that it was my turn to roll. I put a Pass Line bet down. The Darksiders each put a $25 Don't Pass bet down.

On the Come Out roll, the Darksiders are at a distinct disadvantage as they lose when a 7 or 11 is rolled and only win when a 2 or 3 is rolled. That gives them eight chances to lose and only three chances to win. But once the Darksider gets by the Come Out roll, once that shooter has established a point number, then the game turns in his favor with a vengeance. He gets paid even money on bets he is moderately to heavily favored to win.

The man with few teeth shouted from his side of the table: "Knock dem bums outta da game. Seven or eleven!"

I set my dice in the inverted "V" and lofted them to my spot at the end of the table just before the curve.

"Seven! Winner Seven!" shouted the stickman.

The Darksiders had each lost $25. They then put down $50 each. This was a classic Martingale wager—doubling a bet after you lost. It's a dangerous way to play.

I picked up the dice again. I rolled.

"Seven, another seven!" shouted the stickman.

"Yahoo!" shouted the man with few teeth. I could even see that the Captain was smiling. The Darksiders now put up $100 each on the Don't Pass side. Neither looked at me. Nor did they look at anyone else at the table. The man with few teeth was spitting and shouting: "Knock dem bastards out!" The Boxman said to him: "Sir, please."

Then I picked up the dice to roll again. This time I rolled a 4 and that became my point. The Darksiders each put $400 in odds on their Don't Pass bet. They each now had $500 at risk on a single roll of the dice. Whew! They were, of course, hoping that I'd roll a 7 and they would collect $100 for their Don't Pass bet and $200 for their odds bet. There were six chances to roll that 7 and only three chances to roll that 4.

"Son of a bitch, son of a bitch," whispered the man with few teeth.

"Come on," said the Captain, "roll that four."

Somewhere in the part of me that is every bit as superstitious as the most superstitious person on earth was the thought: *Why not have the dealers rooting for a 4 as well?* So I took a five-dollar chip and threw it on the table. "Hard four for the dealers," I said.

I picked up the dice. I really wanted to make that 4, not just for myself, not just for the Captain, not just for the man with few teeth, but for all the right players on earth now and in times to come.

I looked down the end of the table and chanted to myself: *four, four, four!* Then I lofted the dice gently. They bounced once, hit the wall and died. "Four! Four! The easy way! Four! Winner four!" I looked up and I thanked the stars. People at the table cheered. The man with few teeth was sputtering his victory whelps. When I looked down, the two Darksiders had left the table.

Still the Dark Side has its rewards, if played correctly. The Darksiders at my table had made some fundamental errors—and it cost them $500 apiece.

## Successful Dark Side Betting

Before you can become a successful Darksider you have to throw out some of the linear thinking that has dominated craps theory since the first mathematician looked at a craps table and stated emphatically that the Dark Side is the same as the right side only in reverse. Yes, mathematically this is so, but in reality it isn't—unless you have a massive bankroll.

In a roundabout way, here's why the Dark Side can't be played as a mirror image of the right side:

Remember how in school the mathematics you learned proved that the shortest distance between two points was a straight line? And then you grew up, and read some books about the universe and physics, and suddenly you discovered that there are no straight lines in the universe because the *very space itself is curved*? Thus, the straightest possible ruler, measuring the straightest possible line was in reality *a curved ruler* that was measuring a curved perfectly straight line! I'm sure most of you remember the day you heard that shocking news the way you remember the day you were told that Santa Claus didn't exist or that casinos were in the business of taking your money while making you feel happy about it.

These three were momentous moments in all our personal histories, no doubt. The universe is curved; there are no straight lines, there is no Santa. And the casinos want to make money.

Well, it's just that kind of figuring that I am going to employ to set up what I consider to be the best Darksider attack on craps. I am not going to tell you the old bromides of put a Don't Pass bet and back it with full odds. Nor am I going to recite the percentages ad nauseam (because the percentages disprove my idea of how to play!). No, we are going to walk the straight and narrow on the curved space of Darksider betting.

Before going further, let me first pause to alert Darksiders to the dangers of traditional approaches to their favored form of betting. Since you have to take the long end of the bet, (for example, when you are laying odds on the Don't Pass or Don't Come number of 4, you must lay two dollars for every one you hope to win), the rewards come in relatively small increments and a lot of money can be blown (a lot of money!) if you stumble onto a hot shooter. Thus, a losing streak on the Dark Side is difficult to make up by Don't betting for obvious reasons. Because you are laying the long odds, you have to hit those 7s with intense frequency to make up the deficit of a losing streak.

Here's another thing to consider, something I wrote about in *The Captain's Craps Revolution!*: craps is really two distinct and separate games. There is the Come Out game and there is the Post–Come Out game. For right bettors, the Come Out game favors them and the Post–Come Out game favors the casinos. For Darksiders, it is just the opposite. The Come Out is the white-knuckle time as you buck eight possible ways to lose (six on the 7 and two on the 11) and only three ways to win (one on the 2, and two on the 3) in 36 possible combinations of two dice. But once you step off the high dive and enter the Post–Come Out part of the game, you are in the driver's seat because the odds favor the 7—sometimes dramatically—over all the other point numbers. (There are six ways to make the 7 to five ways to make the 6 or 8; four ways to make the 5 or 9; and three ways to make the 4 or 10.) The traditional approach of laying odds on your Don't Pass and/or Don't Come bets is the *wrong* approach to *Wrong* betting despite the mathematical proofs to the contrary. The mathematics of craps looks at the game as a whole and in theory.

My approach looks at the game in segments and in reality. The fact is that once you survive the Come Out, why lessen your advantage by putting more money up at fair odds? You have no edge on the new money you are wagering and you must wager the bigger amount. Why bother? In the long run, you will break even on these odds bets and they will not contribute one whit to any comp points. If the game were just Post–Come Out, you would never consider putting up more money without having an edge. The reason Darksiders do so now is because they have been trained to look at craps as a straight line between the Come Out and the Post–Come Out. It is for the Right bettor, who lessens the house edge on the Post–Come Out by putting fair odds bets up when he faces the horrible house edge during this segment. It isn't for the Darksider who lessens his own edge by doing so. It's two different worlds. Forget the mathematics that tells you to put up more money to decrease the overall edge on the Darkside. If you do this you are risking a bad, perhaps, devastating run that can only be cushioned by a huge bankroll that allows you to slowly creep back on the Don't.

Obviously, in my recommendation to forgo the odds bets on the Don't side, I am going against the basic math of the game which shows clearly that the smallest possible bet on the Don't Pass or Don't Come and the largest possible bet in odds is the best way to go. Indeed, for a small minority of players it is the best way to go if:

1. those players have rather large bankrolls to support taking the long end of bets, and

2. those players are not attempting to get comps.

If you have a huge bankroll and you can withstand a devastatingly bad run on the Dark Side then feel free to bet the traditional ways as they are mathematically superior by a percentage point or so. Keep in mind that you have to win approximately two Dark Side odds bets to make up for every one bet that is lost because you are taking the long end of these bets.

The best Dark Side approach takes into account the fact that most players don't have huge bankrolls and can't afford to come back after a bad run. Why? Because for most players a bad Dark Side run wipes them out. The best Dark Side approach follows the three S formula—Slow, Steady, and Scared.

# The Scobe One-Two

Here's my favorite Dark Side strategy—the Scobe One-Two. That's right, the best Darksider approach to Don't betting has been named after me (who so dubbed this form of betting the Scobe One-Two? I did!) as I am currently its most active, most vocal, and most admiring proponent. I might also be its *only* proponent!

The Scobe One-Two is a straightforward approach to a curved game. Here are the Five Commandments for employing it. The bankroll that you need is 15 times your bet. Thus, if your bet is $10, you will need a $150 session stake to play the Scobe One-Two.

*Commandment 1: You will never risk more than one bet on one shooter.*

*Commandment 2: You will never lose to more than two (different) shooters at the same table.*

*Commandment 3: You will never bet the Don't Pass.*

*Commandment 4: You will only bet the Don't Come.*

*Commandment 5: You will never lay odds bets, unless your bankroll is at least 60 times your bet.*

These rules exist for the purpose of limiting your exposure to any possible hot shooter and also limiting your ability to throw caution to the wind and bet against someone who has previously beaten you because you got upset.

The key to winning at Right betting at craps is to limit your exposure to the casino edge while maximizing your chances for taking advantage of good rolls. The Captain's *5-Count* does this admirably on the Do side of the board. It helps you avoid bad rolls and positions you to take advantage of possible good rolls.

On the Dark Side of the game you want to *avoid* good rolls and you want to position yourself to take advantage of shooters and tables that are cold. Money is usually won slowly on the Dark Side because traditional betting approaches have the player putting a Don't Pass and two or more Don't Come bets with full odds on each shooter. Thus, the traditional Darksider can find himself obliterated during a hot roll because he is putting up more money to win less.

The Scobe One-Two is a real-world method for extending your playing time but not your risk while trying to avoid good shooters. It calls for making only one bet against a given shooter in the following way:

After the shooter has established his point, the Darksider should place a Don't Come bet. If the shooter should roll a 7 or 11, you will, of course, lose. If the losing number was 11, you do not put another bet down against this particular shooter. You wait—for however long it takes—for that shooter to seven out. Feel free to go to another table. If the shooter rolled a 7 (thus, he's sevened out), you repeat the process with the next shooter. You wait for him to establish his point and then you bet just one Don't Come bet. If you should lose on this shooter, you automatically go to another table. That's part of the Scobe One-Two. One bet against one shooter. If two shooters hurt you—you flee!

Of course, if your Don't Come bet should win on the initial roll because the shooter rolled a 2 or 3 then take your winnings, and the original bet back, and wait for another shooter (if you can't wait—reduce your bet in half). On the other hand, if your bet made it to a number and then won because the shooter sevened out, you repeat the process with the next shooter. The Scobe One-Two commands that, win or lose, it's one bet, one shooter. Period.

Whenever you are up on a number, you do not lay any odds unless your bankroll is large in relation to your bet. You have the game heavily in your favor at this point as you are being paid even money for a winning Don't Come bet when in reality you have a two-to-one edge if the number is 4 or 10; a three-to-two edge if the number is 5 or 9, and a six-to-five edge if the number is a 6 or 8. It makes no sense to put up more money at this juncture since that new money is merely a break even game. By not putting up the odds, you'll stretch your limited bankroll.

How does the Scobe One-Two protect you? First, no hot shooter can blow you away since you only make one bet on one shooter. If that shooter should knock you off and continue to roll for the next century, chances are you'll be at another table. If you win on that shooter, you bet against the next shooter as well. Many of your wins will herald another shooter since they will occur when a shooter sevens out. But some won't. Again, you have to have the discipline to only bet once against a given shooter. There is also a good reason why you make only a single Don't Come bet and never put a Don't Pass bet. Often craps players become incensed when they lose and bet manically in a rash attempt to win everything that they lost back.

I have seen the following situation many times at craps tables with Darksiders:

Mr. Darksider comes to the table and places a Don't Pass bet. The shooter rolls a 7. The Darksider ups his bet probably by doubling it. The shooter rolls another 7. The Darksider increases his Don't Pass bet again. Another 7. The Darksider doubles again. An 11. The shooter finally establishes a point. The Darksider then lays full odds (taking the long end of the bet) and Bam! the shooter makes his point. The Darksider again bets Don't Pass (7!), ups his bet (11!), ups his bet (7!), ups his bet (7!). The shooter establishes his second point. The Darksider lays full odds. Bam! The shooter hits his second point. The Darksider is beside himself with grief, while others at the table (all the Right bettors) mock him and snicker at his anguish. You'll recall my experience with the two Darksiders in the beginning of this chapter was similar to the above.

The Darksider who escalates his bets as his emotional turmoil escalates has made a terrible mistake. He has allowed one single shooter to wipe him out. The temptation to continue to stubbornly bet against an individual who has stung you is too great if you allow yourself to go against a shooter on the Don't Pass; whereas on the Don't Come, a single 7 is all you can expect from one shooter, since a single 7 knocks the shooter out as well. Yes, an 11 keeps him in the game—so the 11 opens the door for a second shot at the same shooter. You have to steal yourself and refrain from throwing more money on the table. The Don't Come has more of a built-in restraining influence, whereas the Don't Pass can open us up to going . . . well, berserk.

The reason you leave if you've lost to two shooters is again to limit your exposure to a table that is possibly turning warm because of luck or rhythmic rollers. If two shooters nailed you, walk to another table. While you're walking, you have no money at risk and you aren't setting up the psychological conditions for losing control. At worst, you're licking minor wounds.

The final question to confront on the Dark Side is whether to employ a simple Martingale—a doubling up scheme—after two shooters have knocked you out. If you are betting $25 against a shooter, should you double it against the next shooter in an attempt to get it all back? You'll have to make this decision for yourself. I prefer to simply risk one bet on one shooter, one bet of the same amount on the next. I would rather decrease my bets when things are going poorly than increase them. Yet, a two-step Martingale is not an absurd way to play the Don't side, especially if your first bet is somewhat smaller than your usual bet, and if you refrain from taking it to three, four or more steps when you hit many shooters who are nailing you. I know many Martingale players, it seems to be the most popular betting scheme, and I also know that most of them allow the Martingale mentality to sooner or later run away with them. That's when they double that first bet, then they double the second bet, then they double that . . . until they hit the house limit and hit the deck.

A two-step Martingale would be the preferable way to go if you reduce the size of your first bet. Thus, if you are a $25 player and you bet $15 on the first attempt, lose that and bet $30 on the second attempt, you're total risk on two shooters would be only $45, not $50. This would actually save you money in the long run since you're putting five dollars less into action overall. If you employ the Scobe One-Two exactly as I recommend it, your bankroll will last much longer on the Darkside and you'll never have to worry about one hot shooter, be he a random roller or a rhythmic roller, decimating you.

## Rhythmic Rolling from the Dark Side

I have not given much thought or much practice to rhythmic rolling from the Dark Side of the game. But it is just as likely a phenomenon as rhythmic rolling from the Right side. If you do discover certain dice sets and deliveries that do bring out the 7 more than its one in six probability, then you might want to set up your attack on the casinos with this in mind.

When you roll, start with a Pass Line bet. When you establish your point, Place a No 4 or a No 10 bet. Also Place a "No" bet on whatever the Pass Line point is. Then keep trying for that 7.

Truly sophisticated rhythmic rollers have sets for their Come Out rolls where they try to hit the 7 and, once the point is established, sets and deliveries in order to make specific numbers and avoid the 7.

# Avoid All Golden Shooters!

The *5-Count* on the Right side helps us to avoid bad shooters. Is there a method to avoid good shooters? Yes. Read the section on the Golden Ruler again and remember: these are shooters you, as a Darksider, want to avoid. Anyone who sets the dice carefully and rolls in a controlled fashion is Luke Skywalker to your Darth Vader. Don't go up against them. Pass them by.

# Taking a Walk on the Dark Side of Craps

As an intrepid researcher, I decided to go to Atlantic City and play the Scobe One-Two, which is my own homespun playing strategy for the Dark Side of the line. Truthfully, I wish I hadn't decided to do this because when I got to Atlantic City on Tuesday, April 29th, 1998 I knew that I didn't really want to go through with it.

I am not a Darksider by nature. I prefer to be on the Right side cheering and yelling as shooters make point after point, number after number. The trouble is that very few shooters make number after number and fewer still make point after point.

So I decided to put into practice the method of play that I preach for those individuals who have been taken over by the Forces of Darkness. I would employ the Scobe One-Two.

That would be the strategy, pure and simple, that I planned to employ in Atlantic City. Since there is some lively debate over the principle of laying odds on the Don't, I decided to keep a record of not only my wins and losses in actual play (I was betting $25 per Don't Come wager) but my potential wins and losses (and swings in bankroll) had I laid double odds on the Don't. Since I would be betting $25, I would have to lay $60 to win $50 on the 6 and 8 (total money at risk would be $85); I would have to lay $75 to win $50 on the 5 and 9 (total money at risk would be $100); and I would have to lay $100 to win $50 on the 4 and 10 (total money at risk would be $125). Remember, the odds bets were *mental bets* as I was too cowardly to put this kind of money into play as a part of my Darksider experiment. I would make 100 bets over a four day period, going from casino to casino along the boardwalk.

I was as much, if not more, interested in what it *feels* like to play the Dark Side as I know that when Darksiders come to tables where

I'm playing, I find myself resentful of their presence (yes, yes, I know that they have no influence on the dice and, yes, I know that in reality we are all betting against the house and, yes, I know that my feelings are not based on logic or science but, no, I'm not going to deny how I feel). At the end of this diary is a complete rundown of every wager, the highs and lows, and so forth. You will note that there were wide swings of fortune as Lady Luck either smiled at me or spurned me. Because there were an inordinate number of fours and nines that were made by the various shooters, a remarkable thing occurred—I wound up winning $50 using the Scobe One-Two whereas I would have wound up losing $135 had I laid the odds!

Of course, as any self-respecting gambling writer will admit, 100 decisions isn't even a drop in the bucket of probability and these results actually have no bearing on the discussion of whether or not to lay odds on the Don't side of the game. What you will note, however, is that the amount of the swings when laying odds ($1,055) were proportionally greater than the amount of the swings when not laying odds ($350). If you can handle the downs of such betting, then you can reap the rewards as well. My nature is cautious and I can't handle the downs cavalierly. Whether to lay odds on the Don't is a close call and will probably best be left up to your gambling temperament.

## TUESDAY, APRIL 29TH

It's two o'clock in the afternoon when I arrive at the Showboat Casino in Atlantic City. Showboat is on the Northern tip of the boardwalk and thus is a good starting point for a stroll that takes in all the boardwalk casinos. The furthest Southern casino is the old Bally's Grand, now the "new" Hilton, both of which were once the glamorous Golden Nugget.

Check-in goes smoothly, the line is short and my dinner reservations are confirmed. As I walk away from the check-in counter, I smell the aroma of the casino. No matter how many times I visit casinos throughout America, my heart starts to thump audibly in my chest (I swear—*audibly!*) when I smell that aroma: a delectable commingling of smoke, booze, soft drinks, human pheromones, adrenaline and hope that just gets the blood to boiling. And if you don't control that boiling blood, you'll take a bloody beating at the tables or the machines—that's a given and all you players know this. Ah, but I do love that casino smell.

I'm in my room on the 19th floor. Showboat offers some spectacular views of ocean and city if you get the right rooms. My wife, the beautiful A.P., is not with me on this trip as she had to take care of the business of Paone Press and as she can't stand the thought of betting on the Dark Side for any extended time as I am planning. I miss her already and I've just barely checked in.

The Showboat's rooms are spacious and clean and all casinos should emulate the layouts of their oversized, brightly-lit bathrooms. Although the games at Showboat and all of Atlantic City are nondescript when compared with Las Vegas or Tunica in Mississippi, it's the only game in town for most East Coasters who want a day trip to Lady Luckland. In Atlantic City you can find the occasional craps table with 5X odds, even some with 10X odds, but mostly you'll find double odds; you'll find eight-deck blackjack games with mediocre penetration and some six-deck games in high-roller pits. Most of the tables have high minimums. The five dollar minimum table has almost vanished.

The Showboat casino is relatively bright and very festive and the dealers, for the most part, are professional and friendly. Whenever I'm in Atlantic City I always think to myself—why can't this town be more like Vegas? It's so beautiful with the ocean and sand and boardwalk, why can't AC have many low-minimum tables with 10X or 20X or a 100X odds on craps and also single and double-deck blackjack and better video poker games and looser slots?

Unfortunately, Vegas is becoming more like Atlantic City every day as their new mega-casinos emulate the bad games of the East Coast. To me a good game is a game I can beat. To the casinos, a good game is a game nobody can beat. To me a *decent* game is a game where the casino has less than a 1.5 percent edge. With a low edge such as that, you have a nice shot at winning in the short run but no shot in the long run.

Well, I'm not in Atlantic City to play blackjack, although I probably will find the game with the best penetration and give it a go. In eight-deck games with AC rules (just about all the casinos in AC have the same rules with a few minor variations), the key variable is penetration. If you can get a game where they're only cutting out a deck from play, then when you get five decks into the game, you can have confidence in your count and take it to them at the end, knowing that what is theoretically likely to happen will be really likely to happen with so few cards being kept out of play.

But on this trip, I must think in terms of craps, not blackjack.

My game plan is to play the Dark Side of craps in a rather simple way. I am going to place 25 bets of $25 each on each day for four days. If possible I will play at every casino on the boardwalk and, if the spirit moves me, I'll journey over to Harrah's and Trump's Marina which are both in the Marina section of the city. I will record any interesting events and, truthfully, get this damn experiment over with.

Enough analyzing. I'm going to take a brief nap and then I'm going to start my Darksider Odyssey.

It's four o'clock and I'm at Trump Plaza in the center of the boardwalk. I wanted to take a walk before dinner and I figured I don't have to start on one end of the boardwalk and work my way down. I can play any way and any where I like.

Trump Plaza's casino is on the second floor and it's a long casino.

If I'm going to do this, I'm going to do it. I wonder how it feels to be the odd man out at a craps table?

The very first time I go to the table as a Darksider I have a confrontation! Some relatively attractive woman (I can't bring myself to call her attractive because she had an ugly disposition and a woman's disposition informs her beauty) was at the head of the table—there were eight people at the table—and I moved to her left so I could be close to the Don't Come box and unobtrusively place my bet after the shooter established a point. As soon as I placed my Don't Come bet, she turns to me and says in a rather loud voice: "Do you have to play at this table?" I stammered out: "I'm just placing one Don't Come bet." She again repeated: "Do you have to play at this table?" Only now she said it so loud that everyone at the table and at the next table and throughout the whole world could hear her say: DO YOU HAVE TO PLAY AT THIS TABLE!? I never expected that.

The shooter rolled a 4 on his second roll and my Don't Come went up on the Don't 4—or *behind the line* as they say in craps talk. The 4 was two-to-one in my favor as there are six ways to make the 7 and only three ways to make the 4. Therefore, a 7 I win, a 4 I lose.

The woman had placed a Come bet of $10, the table minimum, and was now backing it with $20. I could feel her hate—it oozed from her pores. The very next roll the shooter hit the 4 and the woman won her bet. Since I was not going to lose twice to the same shooter I waited. The very next roll was a seven-out. The woman snarled at me and left the table.

The next shooter rolled and after he established his point (I didn't keep track of the point numbers as I was only interested in what I was doing), I put another Don't Come bet down. A 6 was rolled and I was put behind the line on the Don't 6. The shooter rolled about three numbers—but no 6—before he sevened out. I was now even. I had won one and lost one at this table. I waited for the next shooter and again put my Don't Come down. I won this too.

Here's the interesting fact. I stayed at Trump Plaza for over two hours waiting to lose two bets in a row! It wasn't until my 21st and 22nd bets that I lost two in a row. What's interesting is that there were several good rolls during this time but, other than my initial loss when the number was hit, they had no bearing on me. After I lost two in a row, I headed back to Showboat and dinner. After dinner, I played three decisions at Showboat, losing once and winning twice. This first day had gone rather well—after a rocky opening with that woman. As I won 16 bets and lost only 9 bets, I was up a nice $175. Had I been laying odds, however, I would have been up $330.

## WEDNESDAY, APRIL 30TH

The gods just love to kick us mortals in the head! Today was the exact reverse of yesterday. I won 9 decisions and lost 16 decisions. I played at three different casinos—Showboat, Taj Mahal, and Resorts which are all linked by walkways. At each casino I could feel a kind of tension at the table when I placed my Don't Come bet; however, no one said anything and no one gave me a dirty look (that I could see, anyway). Maybe I just imagined a tightening of everyone's gut as I entered the game and a joy when I was banged out twice in a row which made me leave a game. Maybe I'm being self-conscious about this Darksider business. Maybe I should grow up and realize that I'm imagining that people are hostile to me at the tables. At the end of the day, I'm even for the trip. Had I been laying odds, I would be up $35. I still sense that people tighten up and I am aware of frowns at the corners of my consciousness . . . or am I?

## *THURSDAY, MAY 1ST*

Grow up? Indeed! I am *emphatically not* imagining the fact that people are uncomfortable when they have Darksiders at the table. At one table at Claridge, three of us were playing the Don't and all the Do players left! A few of these Right siders shot us looks that could kill. That left the three Darksiders just standing there looking at each other because none of us wanted to shoot. One poor guy came to the table, oblivious to the fact that there were three of us hovering like vultures waiting for him to roll. We all pretended to be busy looking around so that he would place his bets—at which point we'd pounce. He put down his $15 Pass Line bet. The other two guys each put $10 Don't Pass bets. He rolled a couple of craps and then got on a number. I then put my Don't Come bet in the square and the other two guys, who were on the opposite side of the table, near the shooter, also put Don't Come bets. The shooter placed the 6 and 8 for $30 each.

It was now that the shooter realized that everyone at the table was betting Don't. He looked at me—I could swear that he was begging me to bet Come instead of Don't Come. The other two vultures were on his side of the table and he made furtive glances in their direction. The poor guy was surrounded. He rolled a number, 10, then promptly sevened out and ran, and I do mean he *ran* from the table. We three vultures eyed each other and I left to go to the Sands which is right next door to the Claridge.

At the Sands, a guy who looked like Jake LaMotta decided he didn't like me and started to blow smoke from a huge cigar into my face. I knew he was doing it on purpose because he had to turn his bull neck to get the smoke to go into my face. I won a couple of decisions so I stayed at the table and took my smoke like a man. Then I lost a couple of decisions and split. I could swear that "Cigar Man" was growling when I left. I wonder if guys such as "Cigar Man" are thoughtful and caring lovers, glib and witty conversationalists, kind and humane human beings? Or do they revert to traveling on all fours when the rest of us can't see them? Does the hotel have to put straw in their rooms for them to nibble and then sleep on?

This third day was not so hot overall. I won 11 decisions but lost 14. I'm now down $75. Had I been laying odds, I would be down $420.

## FRIDAY, MAY 2ND

Twenty-five more decisions to go and then I end this experiment on the Dark Side. I'll head for Tropicana which has 5X odds on all tables although this has no effect on how I'm playing. Trop is the best craps game in AC as of this writing. When I got there I noticed that the blackjack games, which used to be the best in the city, now are the worst. It looked to me like they were cutting three of the eight decks out of play. Even basic strategy players must get irritated waiting for the endless eight-deck shuffle to be completed. The Trop has also been taken over by the machines. What used to be a large lobby has now become a small lobby with a large assortment of slots.

I played five decisions at Trop before moving over to the Hilton, which has what I consider to be the number one restaurant in all of Atlantic City—Peregrines. This is gourmet to top all gourmet and I recommend it highly—provided you have won large pots of money prior to your reservation.

I lost my first two decisions at the Hilton, moved to another table and won five decisions in a row! Then I lost two decisions and left the place for Caesars.

For some strange reason, I have rarely gone into this version of the Caesars' empire. Maybe that's because the first time I did, the place was so dark I could hardly make out what I was doing. This time it was different. I guess the place was relighted or redecorated or my eyesight is better. The place looked great. I lost my first decision there and then won five in a row before losing two.

I went to Bally's Park Place for my last three decisions. At Bally's the last incident with other players occurred. A man was about to roll at the head of the table and I slipped in on his right—I didn't touch him as he was two spaces away and I had positioned myself at the upper reaches of the table, almost on the dealer's side. He rolled a 5, and then I put down my Don't Come bet. He was picking up the dice and then he just dropped them. "No roll," said the boxman. "Get away from my right side," he yelled at me. "You'll give me bad luck unless you're on my left."

I moved over to his left. He rolled a 5 (making his point). I was on the Don't 5 now and he was on his Come Out again. He rolled a seven. Good luck for him and good luck for me. I took my win, finished $50 up for the experiment, and departed.

# CONCLUSIONS

What have I learned? Four days of playing the Dark Side reinforced the fact that craps is one tough game to beat. Right siders always think that the Wrong side somehow wins more often. It isn't so. The distribution of the wins and losses is different but it only *appears* that Darksiders are getting the best of it in the long run. Appearances are deceiving but emotionally telling nevertheless.

It is not a fun way to play. Admittedly I started my quest prejudiced and I ended it biased against playing the Don't. I found it difficult to look at the other players at the table when I knew in my heart that I was rooting for that 7 to show.

I remembered something I discovered when researching my book *Beat the Craps Out of the Casinos: How to Play Craps and Win!*, and that is this: Many players refer to the 7 as the devil. As a Darksider I was rooting for "the devil to jump up" as the saying goes.

Logic, intelligence, gambling savvy all have a tendency to go out the window when mean-looking guys with 24-hour cigars blow smoke at you, and when seemingly pretty women snarl beast-like in your direction, and when grown men run from your presence as if you are bringing the Black Death.

I'll give you inveterate Darksiders credit, however—it takes guts to go with the Devil!

**Scobe's Walk on the Dark Side Daily Tally and Totals**

| *Day 1:* | Don't Come | Number Hit | W/L | Total | W/L + Odds | Total |
|---|---|---|---|---|---|---|
| 1. | 4 | 4 | -$25 | -$25 | -$125 | -$125 |
| 2. | 6 | 7 | +$25 | 00 | +$75 | -$50 |
| 3. | 9 | 7 | +$25 | +$25 | +$75 | +$25 |
| 4. | 2 | — | +$25 | +$50 | +$25 | +$50 |
| 5. | 10 | 10 | -$25 | +$25 | -$125 | -$75 |
| 6. | 3 | — | +$25 | +$50 | +$25 | -$50 |
| 7. | 8 | 8 | -$25 | +$25 | -$85 | -$135 |
| 8. | 3 | — | +$25 | +$50 | +$25 | -$110 |
| 9. | 9 | 7 | +$25 | +$75 | +$75 | -$35 |
| 10. | 7 | — | -$25 | +$50 | -$25 | -$60 |
| 11. | 9 | 7 | +$25 | +$75 | +$75 | +$15 |
| 12. | 6 | 7 | +$25 | +$100 | +$75 | +$90 |

| Day 1: | Don't Come | Number Hit | W/L | Total | W/L + Odds | Total |
|---|---|---|---|---|---|---|
| 13. | 9 | 7 | +$25 | +$125 | +$75 | +$165 |
| 14. | 10 | 7 | +$25 | +$150 | +$75 | +$240 |
| 15. | 8 | 8 | -$25 | +$125 | -$85 | +$155 |
| 16. | 10 | 7 | +$25 | +$150 | +$75 | +$230 |
| 17. | 5 | 7 | +$25 | +$175 | +$75 | +$305 |
| 18. | 10 | 10 | -$25 | +$150 | -$125 | +$180 |
| 19. | 4 | 7 | +$25 | +$175 | +$75 | +$255 |
| 20. | 6 | 7 | +$25 | +$200 | +$75 | +$330 |
| 21. | 11 | — | -$25 | +$175 | -$25 | +$305 |
| 22. | 7 | — | -$25 | +$150 | -$25 | +$280 |
| 23. | 5 | 7 | +$25 | +$175 | +$75 | +$355 |
| 24. | 9 | 9 | -$25 | +$150 | -$100 | +$255 |
| 25 | 6 | 7 | +$25 | +$175 | +$75 | +$330 |

| Day 2: | | | | | | |
|---|---|---|---|---|---|---|
| 26. | 11 | — | -$25 | +$150 | -$25 | +$305 |
| 27. | 9 | 7 | +$25 | +$175 | +$75 | +$380 |
| 28. | 11 | — | -$25 | +$150 | -$25 | +$355 |
| 29. | 4 | 7 | +$25 | +$175 | +$75 | +$430 |
| 30. | 7 | — | -$25 | +$150 | -$25 | +$405 |
| 31. | 9 | 7 | +$25 | +$175 | +$75 | +$480 |
| 32. | 7 | — | -$25 | +$150 | -$25 | +$455 |
| 33. | 5 | 5 | -$25 | +$125 | -$100 | +$355 |
| 34. | 8 | 7 | +$25 | +$150 | +$75 | +$430 |
| 35. | 9 | 9 | -$25 | +$125 | -$100 | +$330 |
| 36. | 6 | 6 | -$25 | +$100 | -$85 | +$245 |
| 37. | 9 | 9 | -$25 | +$75 | -$100 | +$145 |
| 38. | 6 | 7 | +$25 | +$100 | +$75 | +$220 |
| 39. | 10 | 10 | -$25 | +$75 | -$125 | +$95 |
| 40. | 9 | 9 | -$25 | +$50 | -$100 | -$5 |
| 41. | 8 | 8 | -$25 | +$25 | -$85 | -$90 |
| 42. | 7 | — | -$25 | 00 | -$25 | -$115 |
| 43. | 2 | — | +$25 | +$25 | +$25 | -$90 |
| 44. | 11 | — | -$25 | 00 | -$25 | -$115 |
| 45. | 10 | 7 | +$25 | +$25 | +$75 | -$40 |
| 46 | 7 | — | -$25 | 00 | -$25 | -$65 |
| 47 | 5 | 7 | +$25 | +$25 | +$75 | +$10 |

| Day 2: | Don't Come | Number Hit | W/L | Total | W/L + Odds | Total |
|---|---|---|---|---|---|---|
| 48. | 7 | — | -$25 | 00 | -$25 | -$15 |
| 49. | 7 | — | -$25 | -$25 | -$25 | -$40 |
| 50. | 4 | 7 | +$25 | 00 | +$75 | +$35 |

| Day 3: | | | | | | |
|---|---|---|---|---|---|---|
| 51. | 8 | 8 | -$25 | -$25 | -$85 | -$50 |
| 52. | 3 | — | +$25 | 00 | +$25 | -$25 |
| 53. | 8 | 8 | -$25 | -$25 | -$85 | -$110 |
| 54. | 10 | 7 | +$25 | 00 | +75 | -$35 |
| 55. | 9 | 7 | +$25 | +$25 | +$75 | +$40 |
| 56. | 5 | 5 | -$25 | 00 | -$100 | -$60 |
| 57. | 2 | — | +$25 | +$25 | +$25 | -$35 |
| 58. | 9 | 7 | +$25 | +$50 | +$75 | +$40 |
| 59. | 4 | 4 | -$25 | +$25 | -$125 | -$85 |
| 60. | 7 | — | -$25 | 00 | -$25 | -$110 |
| 61. | 8 | 7 | +$25 | +$25 | +$75 | -$35 |
| 62. | 4 | 4 | -$25 | 00 | -$125 | -$160 |
| 63. | 6 | 7 | +$25 | +$25 | +$75 | -$85 |
| 64. | 7 | — | -$25 | 00 | -$25 | -$110 |
| 65. | 7 | — | -$25 | -$25 | -$25 | -$135 |
| 66. | 8 | 8 | -$25 | -$50 | -$85 | -$220 |
| 67. | 7 | — | -$25 | -$75 | -$25 | -$245 |
| 68. | 11 | — | -$25 | -$100 | -$25 | -$270 |
| 69. | 3 | — | +$25 | -$75 | +$25 | -$245 |
| 70. | 4 | 4 | -$25 | -$100 | -$125 | -$370 |
| 71. | 4 | 4 | -$25 | -$125 | -$125 | -$495 |
| 72. | 10 | 7 | +$25 | -$100 | +$75 | -$420 |
| 73. | 3 | — | +$25 | -$75 | +$25 | -$395 |
| 74. | 6 | 7 | +$25 | -$50 | +$75 | -$320 |
| 75. | 9 | 9 | -$25 | -$75 | -$100 | -$420 |

| Day 4 | | | | | | |
|---|---|---|---|---|---|---|
| 76. | 5 | 7 | +$25 | -$50 | +$75 | -$345 |
| 77. | 7 | — | -$25 | -$75 | -$25 | -$370 |
| 78. | 9 | 7 | +$25 | -$50 | +$75 | -$295 |
| 79. | 6 | 6 | -$25 | -$75 | -$85 | -$380 |
| 80. | 8 | 8 | -$25 | -$100 | -$85 | -$465 |

| Day 4: | Don't Come | Number Hit | W/L | Total | W/L + Odds | Total |
|---|---|---|---|---|---|---|
| 81. | 7 | — | -$25 | -$125 | -$25 | -$490 |
| 82. | 6 | 6 | -$25 | -$150 | -$85 | -$575 |
| 83. | 8 | 7 | +$25 | -$125 | +$75 | -$500 |
| 84. | 2 | — | +$25 | -$100 | +$25 | -$475 |
| 85. | 2 | — | +$25 | -$75 | +$25 | -$450 |
| 86. | 10 | 7 | +$25 | -$50 | +$75 | -$375 |
| 87. | 6 | 7 | +$25 | -$25 | +$75 | -$300 |
| 88. | 10 | 10 | -$25 | -$50 | -$125 | -$425 |
| 89. | 11 | — | -$25 | -$75 | -$25 | -$450 |
| 90. | 6 | 6 | -$25 | -$100 | -$85 | -$535 |
| 91. | 9 | 7 | +$25 | -$75 | +$75 | -$460 |
| 92. | 9 | 7 | +$25 | -$50 | +$75 | -$385 |
| 93. | 3 | — | +$25 | -$25 | +$25 | -$360 |
| 94. | 8 | 7 | +$25 | 00 | +$75 | -$285 |
| 95. | 5 | 7 | +$25 | +$25 | +$75 | -$210 |
| 96. | 7 | — | -$25 | 00 | -$25 | -$235 |
| 97. | 10 | 10 | -$25 | -$25 | -$125 | -$360 |
| 98. | 4 | 7 | +$25 | 00 | +$75 | -$285 |
| 99. | 4 | 7 | +$25 | +$25 | +$75 | -$210 |
| 100. | 5 | 7 | +$25 | +$50 | +$75 | -$135 |

**Most Up:** $200 without odds (Day One)   $480 with odds (Day Two)

**Most Down:** $150 without odds (Day Four)   $575 with odds (Day Four)

**Won:** 51 decisions

**Lost:** 49 Decisions

**Most Wins in a row:** 5 (twice) on Day Four

**Most Losses in a row:** 4 on Day Three

**Total Losses to 7 & 11 on initial bet:** 20 (expectation: 23—35/8 = 22.9%—12 push/not included)

**Total Wins to 2 and 3 on initial bet:** 11 (expectation: 9—35/3 = 8.6%—12 push/not included)

**Total:** +$50 without odds   -$135 with odds

# Get the Mathematical Edge on the Dark Side of the Line!

You have probably believed that it is impossible to get a a clear-cut edge at craps—of the mathematical kind that is.

Well, there is a way to get a clear mathematical edge on the Dark Side if you have nerves of steal and a winning disposition. I have even done it a couple of times. How? You *buy* Don't Come bets from the other players once they are up on the numbers.

Here's how it works:

Some players are squeamish when they go up on the Don't Come 6 or Don't Come 8 and often tell the dealers to take their bets down. If such a person is near you, stop him. Offer to return his bet plus a little something extra. Remember that the 7 has a six to five edge over the 6 and 8—not a huge edge but enough to make buying the bet very worthwhile. Say, the player has $30 on the Don't 6. You are a six-to-five favorite to win but you get paid even money—you don't have to pay the long end of the bet—which would be six dollars for five dollars or $25 for a winning $30 Don't Come 6.

Give the guy $33 and ask him if you can take over his bet. You will be paid $30 if the seven shows, when the true odds should have paid you only $27.50. Some players won't even want the extra money—or you can offer them a dollar and they feel contented. Meanwhile you have done what so few people can do—get a mathematical edge on a casino bet!

# Comps from the Dark Side

If you follow my advice and you don't place odds on your Don't Come bets but, rather, buck the 1.4 percent house edge and if you only play one Don't Come bet per shooter, you'll find an interesting thing happening. First, the total amount of your risk per hour will be relatively small for two reasons:

1. Betting on one Don't Come means that the "risk time" will be low because most of the time your money will not be acted upon.

2. If a shooter gets hot, you'll be riding it out without making any bets. Take a look at the following chart and you'll see what I'm talking about. "Risk-time" as I define it is simply how often your

money will be acted upon for a decision during a given part of the Darksider game.

| Number: | Decisions | No Decisions | Time at Risk |
|---|---|---|---|
| Initial Roll | 11 (7, 11, 2, 3) | 25 (all other numbers) | 31% |
| 4 or 10 | 9 (7, 4 or 10) | 27 (all other numbers) | 25% |
| 5 or 9 | 10 (7, 5 or 9) | 26 (all other numbers) | 28% |
| 6 or 8 | 11 (7, 6 or 8) | 25 (all other numbers) | 31% |

I estimate that you will be involved in approximately 30 decisions per hour, as opposed to the 60 or more decisions most Darksiders face when they go up on two or more numbers or consistently go against a shooter who is beating them. Even if you *witness* 120 rolls in a given hour (that is two rolls a minute—a good pace), you will not have a bet decided (or even active) on very many of them—probably no more than 25 percent. Yet, you'll be at the table, adrenaline pumping, anticipation soaring, and comps climbing.

The casino raters will usually figure you to be involved in approximately 60 decisions per hour, as that is a general casino rule of thumb from what I can ascertain. If you are betting $25 per shooter, the casino will have your total action as $1,500 per hour or $6,000 for four hours. At a 1.5 percent edge (the low end of the comp equation), the casino will figure your theoretical loss at $90 for that time. In reality, your theoretical loss will be around $42 because you are only putting into action $3,000 with a 1.4 percent house edge. If the casino gives back 40 percent of your theoretical loss ($90) in comps, you're only slightly behind in the *total game* to the tune of six dollars! (Because 40 percent of the $90 is $36.) If the casino gives back 50 percent in the form of comps, you'll be ahead by three dollars.

Of course, I can't state without any reservations what any given casino will do. But my experience tells me that a person who bets $25 on the Don't at craps, and plays an average of four hours per day, tends to get discounts on rooms and food that add up to much, much more than $36 in value. Regardless, the point is clear; in the total game vs. the casino, you are better off betting one Don't Come per shooter and not using the odds option. If you are betting Don't Pass with odds and your total betting action comes to $3,000 as in the example above, your theoretical loss is approximately $18 (figuring double odds)—without the benefit of comps. Remember that almost no casinos count the odds portions of your bets in their comping formula and on the Don't side a hefty amount of the money you'd put into action if you availed yourself of the odds option would be—*on the odds option*! If you are staying at a casino for a few days, and not just passing through with no intention of asking for a comp, then you must look at what you are doing in terms of the *total game* against the casino. Comps factor in that total game.

Naturally I recognize that the purest mathematical strategy from the Don't point of view is to play the traditional Don't Pass and/or Don't Come and take the odds. But when we are staying at a casino, our war isn't solely against the house edge, it's against the house itself. What is the point of losing "only" $18 if you have to pay five times that amount for your room and three times that amount for your food? Isn't it better to have a theoretical loss of $42—and get the comps? In some scenarios, as witnessed by the above, indeed it is.

# TEN

# Protect Yourself at All Times

There are two ways to lose your money in a casino. You can have bad luck when the casino defeats you, or you can have even worse luck when some criminal steals whatever money you might have won after you had good luck.

One day on the boardwalk outside Trump's Plaza in Atlantic City, the Captain saw an elderly woman who was crying. He went up to her to see what was the matter. She told him that she had just come from the ladies' room in the casino where her pocketbook was stolen while she was in the stall. "I hung it up on the door and this hand reached over and just took it," she told the Captain. She screamed but whoever had relieved her of her purse was quick as a deer and was long gone by the time anyone knew what had transpired. "I had just won $500, too," she lamented. "I'm 82 years old," she said, "my husband's deceased, my children are all moved away, and this is the best luck I had in years." Then she cried some more. The Captain had his limo take her to her home in Brooklyn.

Also in Atlantic City, I was entering the lobby of the Claridge from the side door one evening when I saw one guy bump a lady and, when she turned to see who had bumped her, another guy open her purse and take out her wallet so fast that as I was simultaneously opening the door and my mouth to yell "Watch out!"—the two of them were out the front door and into the night. I ran to the front door, exited, and looked to see where they were headed but they were gone . . . vanished into wherever evil vanishes. When I reentered the lobby, the lady didn't know what had happened until I told her that some crooks had grabbed her wallet from her purse. "I didn't feel anything," she lamented. "How did it happen?" I explained. "One guy bumped you and one guy robbed you." She filed a report.

In Las Vegas, several blocks north from today's Stratosphere Tower (then Vegas World), my wife, the beautiful A.P., and I had taken our clothes to a laundromat to be cleaned. We walked from the Sahara, where we were staying, and dropped the clothes off at the place, and started to walk back. Now, this was during a time when A.P. had decided to make all of our clothing and we were wearing matching flower-print shirts and we just looked so damned cute in our matching outfits. Two huge bruisers sleepy-eyed us as we passed them and, from years of living in New York my antennae went up, I thought we might be in trouble—because we did look so damned cute in our matching flower-print outfits. Cute enough to be perfect mugging victims. So I did what I always do when I think someone might mean me harm—I turned and looked them square in the eyes and then I *knew* we were in trouble! These guys started towards us, they were maybe 30 feet away. I whispered to A.P. to run across the street (Las Vegas Blvd.) when I gave the signal. I waited for the cars that had been stopped at the light to get to a certain point and then, when they did I gave A.P. the subtle signal—I shouted "Run!"— and we ran like hell across the street. The brutes tried to run after us but the cars came and prevented them. We kept running until we reached the Sahara.

The above incidents are not that strange for Atlantic City, or Las Vegas or any other venue where gambling attracts those of *us* who wish to fleece Fortune and those of *them* who wish to fleece us. [In fact, such incidents are not strange for any tourist venue or shopping mall for that matter.] Yet, some casino games and some casino-hotel locales lend themselves much more readily to criminals preying upon us than do others. Gaming readers get great advice in many books about the various strategies for handling the various games, but how do you handle the variety of criminals that prey upon those games in a variety of ways? How do you stop criminals from having an edge over decent citizens in casino-hotels? Here's how:

1. *Pocket Watch.* In a casino, men, you should never keep your wallets in your back pockets. Get a shirt with a pocket in front that buttons and keep your money in there. Some savvy craps players even keep a "dummy" wallet in their back pockets. The Captain does this. He keeps his money in his front shirt pocket, double-buttoned, but he has a nice big, fat wallet in his back pocket as well. He figures that if he's confronted by a thief inside a casino, the thief will automatically go for the wallet, get it and run. If the Captain's wallet is stolen, the criminal finds himself with shredded paper instead of big bills and a note that reads: "Why don't you get a real job, creep?"

2. *Purse Position.* In a casino, women, never put your purse on the floor, or on the drink shelf that surrounds the craps table at thigh level, or between slot machines. Doing so is an invitation to long-armed thieves. Keep your purse wrapped securely around your shoulder. Some blackjack tables now come equipped with a "purse holder" that fits into the space between the felt and the cushion. You can wrap your purse strings around it and anyone trying to take it will have to steal the entire table as well. Or keep your purse on your lap covered by your arm, or keep it in your hands. The bottom line is to make the thief realize that it is going to take quite an effort to dislodge you from your purse.

3. *Strapped for Cash.* Women, for casino, hotel and tourist purposes get a small pocketbook that you double strap to your shoulder whenever you go for a stroll. In fact, if you have a coat, always keep your purse under your coat so that any would-be purse snatcher has to get through the coat first. Wrap the straps around your arm twice. By double strapping your purse, anyone who tries to take it will have to take you with it. The beautiful A.P.'s Aunt Katherine has an odd ploy that she has developed to confuse would-be purse snatchers. She usually carries *three* pocketbooks! The purse snatcher only has a one in three chance of getting the right one and the right one is usually under her coat!

4. *Chip Arrangements.* Craps players of either sex: when you arrange your chips in the rack in front of you, do so as the casino

does—put your highest denomination chips in the center, your lowest on the ends, and everything else in between. Always ask for $10 worth of one-dollar chips and put five on one end and five on the other end. If you have two racks, ask for $20 and put five and five, five and five. Railbirds—which is what those predators are called who try to steal chips from unsuspecting craps players usually while the player is shooting—take the chips that are on the outside. It is very difficult to remove chips in the center of the chip rack as these are tightly bunched together and right in front of you. Chances are railbirds won't be interested in your dollar chips and will move on. Blackjack players, you should put small-denomination chips on top of large-denomination chips. This will prevent "palmers" from being able to get to the big money when they distract you.

5. *Beware the Watchers.* Don't let strangers watch the game from over your shoulder. For example, craps is a game that normally attracts onlookers. But if someone is getting too close to you, just ask the floorperson to tell the individual to move back. Usually thieves don't like to have any attention paid to them and they will quickly move on. Alerting the floorperson will also give you a pair of eyes that can look the folks behind you square in the face.

6. *Eyeball Their Eyeballs.* Never be afraid to look someone in the eyes. Thieves love the fact that most of us are shy about really eyeballing other people. They realize that most human prey are leery of looking folks square in the face as this is an aggressive, perhaps challenging attitude. And that is just the kind of attitude you want to have in a casino or casino-hotel. If you think someone is eyeing you, or following you, or getting too close to you—turn and look him dead in the face. In fact, make it obvious that you are trying to *remember* his face! Unless the individual is a psychopath who is intent on killing you whether you know what he looks like or not (in which case it doesn't matter if you look at him or don't look at him), most criminals don't want to be seen and will quickly scurry into the woodwork when you eyeball them.

7. *Don't Get Taken for a Ride.* Never get into an elevator with someone who makes you think: "Should I get into the elevator with this person?" If you feel the least bit uncomfortable, if a single hackle goes up, *don't get in*! Many women I know ignore that little voice that says to them: "Don't get into the elevator with that guy." Instead,

they rationalize, "I'm just being paranoid because of the person's race, or ethnicity, or dress. He'll feel bad if he knows I didn't get in the elevator because of him." The hell with *his* feelings! It's *your* safety that is of paramount concern. If the person's dress, or look, or carriage, or comportment, or anything about that person makes you a little fearful, then let him (or her) get into the elevator and you take the next one. It is better to hurt someone else's feelings than to chance being assaulted and having your purse or wallet stolen, or worse, your body and soul traumatized. I believe that nature has given us a sixth sense when it comes to danger but most of us ignore it to our obvious peril. Trust in your feelings when it comes to danger. The worst that can happen if you are mistaken is some guy's feelings are hurt and you get to your room a few minutes later than you planned.

8. *Up Against the Wall.* When you are in the elevator, try to be up against the back wall, or against the side wall. You want to be able to see everyone clearly. Jimmy P., a member of the Captain's Crew, had his wallet lifted in an elevator. "I didn't even know it was gone until I got to the room. I knew I had it when I got into the elevator. When I got into the room it was gone. The elevator was crowded too and I was pressed up against the front door."

9. *Hand to Money.* If someone bumps you, jostles you, or even rubs gently against you, immediately grab the pocket where your wallet is, or grab your purse. Then look to see what's going on. The quick reflex must always be hand to money!

10. *Valet is the Way.* Always use valet parking, even if you have to pay for it. This was dramatically brought home to me when I saw video of a man who was assaulted in the Mirage parking garage, a well-lit, relatively secure facility. In fact, the cameras picked up the assault with graphic detail. I think security even caught the perpetrator. But that didn't lessen the effects of the bad guy's punches as he pummeled his innocent victim, nor the lifelong trauma such a victim experiences having once been used as a heavy bag. It's much better not to be mugged than to have your mugger get caught!

11. *Yell "Fire!" in a Crowded Building.* If you are already on your floor and walking down the hall and someone accosts you, do not yell for help. Instead, yell "FIRE!" at the top of your lungs. Very few people will physically put themselves on the firing line for someone who is being mugged, but almost everyone will run out of their

rooms if they think a fire is occurring. Just keep yelling "Fire! Fire! Fire!"

12. *Knock on Any Door.* If you are walking down your hotel hallway and you are suspicious of the individual trailing you, stop, and knock on the door of whatever room you stopped in front of. Then knock on the door next to it. And on the one next to it. You might even mutter: "I forgot which room we're all in." Just keep knocking on doors. Some are bound to have people answer. It's a rare mugger who will wait around to see which room you really have. Muggers usually like to do their nastiness in silent secrecy.

13. *Don't Trust a Key Check.* Do not assume just because a casino-hotel posts security at the downstairs elevators that you are in fact secure. Some casinos make you show your room key before letting you on the elevators. This gives many an unwary hotel guest a false sense of security. It is not too difficult to get a hotel key for any hotel in Vegas, Atlantic City, or anywhere USA. The casinos rarely change their plastic key design, just the combination that opens the individual doors of the rooms. Even though a key found last week by a criminal won't open any doors, it will open the hotel floors to him. That's all he needs. Once he passes security, the hotel is his. In crowded casinos, such a bad guy will enter the elevator banks with a crowd of people, flash the outdated key, enter the elevator, notice the weakest-wealthiest prey and get off at that person's floor with him or her. So use that same sixth sense of yours when deciding to get on the elevator with individuals even if they have passed the security check point by showing a key.

14. *They Look Like What They Are.* One of the good things about most criminals of the street variety is that they *look like* criminals of the street variety. If you notice someone who looks like a criminal, assume he is a criminal. If you notice that he is headed where you are headed, then head somewhere else. If he heads that way, you head another way—right to the security desk. Chances are the guy tailing you will head elsewhere when he realizes your dodge.

15. *Box It.* If you are bringing cash to a casino, never leave it in your room. Get a safe-deposit box when you check in and leave the bulk of your gambling stake in there. Take out only what you intend to use for the first session of play and for incidental things such as tips.

16. *Security is Your Blanket.* If you have a big night at the tables and are staying at the casino, ask to have a security guard take you to your safe-deposit box or escort you to your room. That is one of their jobs and most casinos will even recommend that you have security escort you. If you have won loads of cash and are headed for your car (at valet!) also have security escort you to the valet parking area. You should offer to tip them when they perform these services.

Individuals who have won big have been robbed right on the casino floor. The Doctor, a member of the Captain's Crew of high rollers, had $12,000 stolen from him just as he left the casino cage. "Someone slammed into me as I was counting up my money. Then, as I tried to balance myself, someone else ripped the bills right out of my hands. Before I could say anything, I was on the floor, without my money, and the two guys were running out the door."

Had the Doctor asked security to escort him to the cage, there's a good chance the crooks would have gone away and looked to rob another day.

17. *Credit Check.* Most casinos are more than happy to extend you a credit line, which is essentially an interest-free loan of money to play the casino's games and you will have anywhere from one week to 45 days to repay it. Getting credit is easy: ask for an application; fill it out, and return it. You'll be informed within a week or two of how much the casino will give you in credit and any other particulars you need to know. Then when you go to a table you just say: "Marker please." It beats carrying cash and it's better than a loan from those nasty advance machines which charge an arm and a leg and one of your children in interest. A marker is an interest free loan from the casino to you. Of course, you have to pay it back, win or lose, but it is a convenience that all players should consider.

18. *Checks Play.* If you don't want to carry cash and you don't want to establish credit but you do want to play for substantial sums of money, then bring travelers checks to the casino. Cash as many as you have to in order to play your first session. Travelers checks are better than cash because if they are lost or stolen, you can get your money back.

19. *What's Yours Could Become Theirs.* At a craps table, always be aware of what bets you have in action. Some brazen thieves like to snatch winning bets from neighboring players. This can easily occur

as many dealers place the winning bets on the felt in the proximity of the winning player, not directly in front of him. A crook can just reach down and grab the win and pretend it is his. If you aren't aware that you have just won a bet, the thief can actually get away with this ploy. If you make a small scene ("Hey, that's my bet!"), the thief will just pretend he got confused. By the way, often in this situation the adjoining player did become confused . . . so don't assume when this happens it really is a calculated attempt to steal—but also don't let him get away with it! Know what bets you have in action at all times.

20. *You Aren't Irresistible.* Men, if a beautiful woman (or even a not-so-beautiful woman) approaches you in a casino and expresses great admiration for your wit, attire, looks, expression, or inner beauty (and the amount you are betting), she's either a hooker or a crook. No man can be witty from afar and no man is so devastatingly personable that women can read his inner spirit from across a room. Women who aggressively approach men in casinos should send up a red flag of caution in you: Halt! Continuing this conversation might lead to bodily injury due to disease or a lessening of one's bankroll due to diswalleting.

21. *Bathroom Blues.* Beware the bathrooms, where no casino cameras can survey the area, and where thieves come to do their dirty. The bathrooms of casinos rarely have security guards. Attendants are present in the better hotels but they are there to see that the bathroom stays clean, not to prevent patrons from getting cleaned out by criminals. Learn a lesson from the woman whose purse was stolen because she hung it up on the bathroom stall. Don't assume some long-armed thief won't reach over and grab your money when you are in no position to stop them. Thankfully, many of the newer casinos and the remodeled bathrooms have shelves by the toilet paper where you can put your purse, or they have hooks that are midway on the door. And men at urinals are not so safe either. In Atlantic City a gang of brazen thieves had a rather nasty modus operandi. They would target senior citizens who had just won some money and were on their way to the bathroom. They would sneak up behind the poor guy while he was at the urinal, put him in a stranglehold, leave him unconscious on the bathroom floor, minus his wallet, his chips, his jewelry and his dignity. There's little enough dignity in a bathroom as it is, there is none when you wind up in this situation. This ring was broken up in 1998 but that doesn't mean other enterprising *uri-*

*nologists* might not attempt to continue the tradition. So men, you should seriously consider going into stalls for all bodily functions and give the urinals a wide berth.

22. *Talk Before You Walk.* Don't assume that because the casino-hotel looks safe and nonthreatening, the neighborhood it's in is equally safe and nonthreatening. My wife A.P. and I love to walk and when we are staying in an unfamiliar town we generally map out a five to six mile walk that we can take every morning. Before we do this we ask someone at the front desk about the surrounding area. Are there any places we shouldn't walk? In Atlantic City, for example, you are better off walking on the boardwalk then through the neighborhoods. In Vegas, your downtown walks should be confined to circuits of the Fremont Street Experience as the surrounding neighborhood will have more hoods than neighbors. Even the Strip isn't as safe as it used to be. I was accosted by a deranged preppie-looking mugger at 5:30AM on the walk outside Mandalay Bay just two days before writing this sentence. Luckily I was able to run down the winding walkway, past the cascading waterfalls, and to the front door where bellhops and valets were clearly visible. My erstwhile mugger didn't follow me. So if you like to walk, then make it a point to talk to casino personnel who can tell you where to go and where not to go.

23. *Spill Grab.* If someone spills a drink at your table, don't just jump up to avoid the splash—grab your chips too! A common ploy for some criminals is to "accidentally" spill a drink, then in a frenzy to prevent it from getting all over the table, they knock over everyone's chips, palming some in the process. If a drink spills, grab first, jump up second.

24. *Buckets in Tray.* When you play slot machines, if you are the type of person who likes to keep a nice full bucket of coins, keep it in the tray in front of you. If someone should come up on your left or right to talk to you immediately put your hand on your bucket. The coin stealers generally work in pairs this way: one talks, while the other walks away with your bucket.

25. *Trust No One.* The protagonist on the hit show *X-Files*, Fox Mulder, was an FBI agent whose credo was to "Trust No One." In a casino that credo translates into great advice. My Aunt Annie put a twenty-dollar in a bill changer that rejected it. She didn't know that

the bill had been rejected or that this particular machine was reject-
ing bills left and right, because a woman started to talk to her just as
she placed the bill into the receptacle. When she turned around to
play her "credits" there were no credits as the machine had spit out
the twenty-dollar bill. Unfortunately, there also was no twenty-dollar
bill either as the woman she had been talking to—or an accomplice—
had taken the rejected twenty! *Trust no one.* The friendly person who
will watch your credit-ladened machine while you go to the bathroom; the person who informs you that you dropped a couple of
quarters on the floor; the person who pardons himself profusely after
bumping you; the lady who asks for the time—are all occasions for
concern. Keep your hands on your wallet, and keep your eyes on
your bucket or chips.

Most casinos have excellent security forces, but no security system in the world is foolproof, and it is equally important that you
take some measure of responsibility for taking care of yourself. While
the chances that you will be a victim are remote, always assume that
you are in a den of thieves. Be prepared. It's tough enough bucking
the house edge on the table games and on the one-armed bandits
without having to buck the those two-legged bandits as well!

# ELEVEN

# Questions and Answers

This chapter is devoted to answering many of the questions I've been asked over the years. Some of these questions are generic in nature, which means so many people have asked them, I can't remember them all. Some are specific letters from individuals that are typical of a type of question I'm often asked. In those cases I have included the name and/or initials of the letter writer along with the letter.

*In my local casino, they have a new game called "Never Ever Craps" where you can't lose on the Come Out to the 2, 3 or 12, instead these become your point. On the Pass Line you don't win on the 11, this also becomes your point. However, you still win on the 7. This seems like an incredible game that gives the players the edge. Does it?*

No. In fact, just the opposite, the player faces a greater house edge than in regular craps. Nor is this version of craps very new. It used to be called Crapless Craps when it was first "invented" at the now defunct Las Vegas World Casino. It was a game designed to soak the suckers and as such it was (and is) no bargain. The house has a 5.38 percent edge on the Pass Line and Come bets at this version of the game. In regular craps the edge is only 1.41 percent—a huge difference. The fact that you can't lose on the Come Out roll to a 2, 3, or 12 is more than offset by the fact that instead of having a sure winner on the 11 during a Come Out (which means a sure winner once every 18 Come Out rolls), the 11 now becomes a loser on 17 of the 18 times it is the point. That's where the house gets your money! So Crapless Craps by any other name—and casinos all over the country keep reinventing this game by giving it new and more fanciful names—is never as good a game as regular craps.

*Some casinos allow 'put" bets. You can place a Pass Line bet after the point has been established and then place the full odds behind them. In Tunica, casinos will allow "put" bets with 20X odds. That means you can "put" five dollars on the Pass Line with $100 in odds. If you win, the Pass Line is paid off at even money but the $100 is paid off at the correct odds. Is this a better game than simply Placing the numbers?*

Most casinos allowing double-odds on Pass and Come bets allow "put" bets because these heavily favor the house due to the even-money payoff on the "line" portion of the bet. Remember that the only reason the casino has such a small edge on the Pass Line has to do with the fact that the player is a two-to-one favorite during the Come Out roll because he wins on the eight combined appearances of the 7 and 11 and only loses on the four combined appearances of the 2, 3 and 12. In a double-odds game, the "put" bet is not superior to Place betting. For example, if you place a $10 "put" bet with $20 odds on the 4 and 10, you win $50 when it hits. However, had you merely Placed the 4 and 10 for $30, you would have won $54! On the 5 and 9, a "put" bet of $10 with $20 odds wins you $40, but a traditional Place bet of the 5 and 9 for $30 wins you $42. On the 6 and 8, a "put" bet of $10 with $20 odds, wins you $34, whereas a traditional Place bet of $30 wins you $35. As you can see the "put" bet at double-odds games is worse than Place betting at such games.

However, when we deal with 20X odds games, the "put" bets are indeed much better than the traditional Place bets even though they are not without an edge for the casino. Let's see why.

In Tunica a "put" bet of five dollars with $100 in odds on the 4 or 10 means that you will lose $630 when the seven shows ($105 X 6) and win $615 when the four or 10 shows (205 X 3). Net loss is $15. House edge is 1.59 percent. The traditional place bet comes in with an edge of 6.67 percent on the 4 or 10. Note that the buy bet at casinos where you only pay commissions when the bet wins has a slightly lower house edge of 1.28 percent!

On the 5 and 9, you will lose $630 when the seven shows and win $620 when the 5 or 9 shows. Net loss is $10. House edge is 0.95 percent. The traditional Place bet comes in with an edge of four percent on the 5 and 9. This is also a significant difference.

On the 6 and 8, you will lose $630 when the seven shows and win $625 when the 6 or 8 shows. Net loss is $5. House edge is 0.43 percent. The traditional Place bet comes in with a house edge of 1.52 percent, again a decided difference.

It is markedly evident that the Tunica "put" bets are far superior to their Place betting counterparts at traditional craps. However, are they better than the standard Pass/Come with double odds? Not quite. The house edge on a double-odds game is 0.61 percent—slightly worse than the Tunica "put" bet of the 6 and 8 and somewhat superior to the "put" bets of 4, 5, 9 and 10. However, in Tunica and other regions, you can take 20X odds as of this writing and here the "put" bets pale by comparison. If you compare a 20X odds game, the Pass/Come player taking full odds at traditional craps faces a mere 0.11 percent house edge. So while you are correct in assuming that the 20X "put" bet was far superior to Place bets, it still lags behind the traditional Pass/Come with odds.

For rhythmic rollers who know which numbers they hit with greater than normal frequency, the "put" bets at 20X odds could be the bet of choice. With extremely low house edges to buck, players who can control the dice and diminish the appearance of the 7 will make more money by "putting" them on the numbers, than placing them on the numbers—at 20X odds games . . . and if you can afford them.

*Who was the biggest high roller you ever saw at craps? Who was the biggest high roller you ever played with?*

Although I've heard about high rollers betting in the hundreds of thousands, the biggest one I ever saw was also the biggest one I ever played with. At The Venetian, A.P. and I played at a craps table with a player I call Megaman because of the size of his bets. His average bet per roll was over $50,000 spread across every number except the 7. Yes, over $50,000 as in the starting yearly salary for teachers in Nevada is around $26,000; as in the starting salary for the Assistant District Attorney in New York City is around $35,000; as in—as in God that is a helluva lot of money to be throwing away on Hardways, Yo-elevens, Snake Eyes, Box Cars and Hop bets.

He was a generous player, too. His tips for the dealers were often purple chips ($500) and his tips for the players who had good rolls were often twice that. But he was loud and something of brat.

It was a $5 minimum table and everyone knew that when it was your turn to shoot, a good roll meant a fortune could be coming your way. Since I was in the midst of a series of good rolls (and have been for several years), I knew my gravy train was standing right across the table from me.

As A.P. and I got to the table, a new shooter had just been given the dice. The Megaman put up a $3,000 Pass Line bet. When the shooter established his point, Megaman put $10,000 in odds behind it and then covered all the numbers with place bets—$4,800 each on the 6 and 8; $5,000 each on the 4, 5, 9 and 10. It didn't matter to him that he was covering his point with a place bet. He then put $1,500 on all the hardways and a couple of hundred on each of the one-roll proposition bets. And we were off!

The shooter immediately hit the hard ten. The Megaman made $10,500 on that. He pressed his hard 10 to $3,000 and the shooter came right back with a second hard 10! That was $21,000. In two rolls Megaman had just won $32,500! Yeow! Megaman turned to the shooter and gave him a yellow chip—$1,000—as a tip. He then threw out a purple chip for "any 10" on the hop for the dealers. My mouth was watering. I couldn't wait to get the dice into my hands. The shooter then promptly sevened out.

## THE STICKMAN AND THE PIT BOSS

It was now the time for Megaman to roll. And roll he did. He must have made about five points and many, many numbers (he filled two chip racks with yellow, $1,000 chips) when the time came for the dealers to rotate and take their breaks. "Whoa!" yelled Megaman, "Hold up! There's to be no change in the stickman when a shooter is rolling. That's my deal with [he named a name I didn't catch]. There's no change!"

The old stickman who, along with the other dealers, had benefitted greatly by Megaman's largesse, hesitated. You could see he didn't know whether to leave or stay.

It was now up to the pit boss who had been carefully watching the game. In fact, he was one of about eight million casino executives congregated on the pit side of the table watching Megaman's action, all strangely happy that they didn't have to make the decision about the stickman.

I whispered to A.P.: "The pit boss is insane if he changes the stickman. This guy will lose a fortune the way he plays. He's a gold mine. I'd do whatever he wants."

The pit boss was a relatively young man with perfectly groomed hair, perfectly fitting suit, and perfectly suited attitude but now he was on the spot.

"Change them," he said, indicating that the stickman take a break.

"That's it!" screamed Megaman, "You guys want me to lose!"

The pit boss snickered but Megaman didn't see it. "I'm going to bring you to your knees," shouted Megaman.

"Not the way he's playing," I said to A.P. "Can you imagine what he'd be able to do if he played the *5-Count*? If he made only the best bets? He'd still get the royal treatment and he'd be able to have a shot at them."

But Megaman now had the dice. He sevened out immediately. He then picked up all his chips and threw them—*threw them*—across the table, and shouted: "I had a deal with [that name again] and you," he pointed to the pit boss, "you are responsible. I'll never play in this stinking casino again. No wonder you guys are dying—you have no idea, not a clue, how to treat players. I had a deal, and you broke it!" He was screaming now. A large crowd was gathered around the table to see what all the shouting was about.

"I don't know of any deal, *sir*," said the pit boss. The young pit boss was trying to act cool but I could see he was shaken. That cool demeanor, that patronizing "sir" that he had practiced on five- and 10-dollar players who were miffed at this or that, couldn't hold up against a player who could change the bottom line for The Venetian in a day or two of play—change it for the Venetian's benefit.

"You damn morons!" screamed Megaman.

Then it was my turn to roll. I had a good roll. About 10 minutes long. I hit a bunch of numbers, made several points, hit a lot of hardways. Megaman wasn't playing. When he finally noticed that I was having a good roll, he put $500 on the Hard 6 for the dealers and said: "I'll press this several times until. . ."

I sevened out!

I came back the next day and Megaman was still there. Evidently, the bosses of the Venetian had assuaged his anger. In fact, he did have a deal with the Venetian that no stickman was to be changed during his roll and also that the dice were to be returned to the shooter as they had fallen on the previous roll. I got to roll three times with Megaman playing. In three weeks of playing craps every day during that particular trip, I had only five rolls where I sevened out immediately after establishing my point—three of them were the three times I rolled with Megaman at the table. I could console myself with the fact that, on all three rolls with Megaman, I was rolling from an unaccustomed spot on the table (I prefer being to the immediate right of the stickman as I've written). I would never have rolled from the far curve of the table had I not hungered for some of Megaman's booty.

In the several days that Megaman played at Venetian, according to one dealer, he lost well over a million dollars. He gave the dealers tens of thousands in tips. He generated excitement and drew crowds. He made the Venetian a happening place while he played. And again, he lost over a million dollars. Now, would you change a stickman on such a cash cow? He's the biggest I ever saw, and the biggest I ever played with.

*I recently received a mailing from a systems seller that promises me a three to one advantage over the casino at craps. He claims that I can win an*

*average of $50 or more an hour using his system and he guarantees it. It's*
*very expensive. Should I buy it?*

I was looking up the titles of craps books and pamphlets recently and I was amazed at how many have been written about the game
over the years—well over 500! Now, my own personal library has
some 30 craps books and pamphlets ranging from excellent to awful.
Most of the books are honest explorations of the math of the game
and recommendations for playing against that inevitable house edge.
There is no earth-shattering information in any of them. Others are
basically idiosyncratic explorations of an individual player's ideas
and experiences.

But some books and many pamphlets promise more than they
can deliver and these usually come with titles that guarantee a win
based on misleading statements. For example, the tome explains that
the system recommended will give the player a three-to-one advantage over the house. At first glimpse this sounds incredible. If getting
such an edge were truly possible, I would own all of Las Vegas in
short order and that would be just for starters. I would in rapid succession put down payments on Atlantic City, Mississippi, the rest of
the United States and then the very earth itself!

Of course, the fact that the author was promising that I could get
a three-to-one advantage was an equivocation—a statement
designed to mislead me into thinking of my future one way (visions
of grandeur), while the writer was actually thinking of me in quite
another way (sucker!).

Here was the system. Once the shooter established his point, I
was to bet $44 inside. I would then have $10 on the 5, $12 on the 6,
$12 on the 8, and $10 on the 9. There are 18 ways for me to hit any of
those four numbers (eight ways to win on the 5 and 9, and ten ways
to win on the 6 and 8). There were only six ways for me to lose on the
7. So 18 ways to win, six ways to lose equals a three-to-one advantage
for me. I would only lose once for every three wins I had. It certainly does sound good.

But if you look closely at the actual bets involved and how they
are paid off, that three-to-one advantage puts me in a very bad position against the casino. Here's why. On the three bets I win, I win a
total of $42 because, whichever numbers hit, I get paid $14 and 3 X 14
= 42. However, when I lose, I don't just lose a bet on one number, I
lose *all four* numbers. So when the 7 shows its ugly head I lose $44!

Follow the math trail and you see that my three-to-one advantage is not a "monetary" advantage but a "decisions" advantage. I will definitely win more decisions in the long run but I will also lose more money as well. The author of this system must have known this fact but he chose instead to make it appear that the edge was a monetary one. He also chose to make it appear that he had discovered a "new way" to bet that would give me a way to beat the casinos.

I have one pamphlet, mimeographed with blue ink, that is very, very old and it purports to show me how to win 80 percent of my bets at craps. It is just a variation of the above only with a more dangerous $64 bet on six numbers. Yes, by betting $64 across ($10 on the 4, $10 on the 5, $12 on the 6, $12 on the 8, $10 on the 9 and $10 on the 10) I will win a whopping 24 times for every six times I lose. In those 24 wins, I will accumulate $360 but in those six losses I will lose $384 for a net loss of $24. Not good.

Some of the more outrageous pamphlets purport to show us how to win 99 percent of our "betting sequences" at craps and other games such as baccarat and roulette. And, in fact, these systems do just that—but we still wind up losing in the long run. Here's how that is accomplished.

By utilizing a Martingale betting system which calls for doubling up a bet after a loss, you can indeed win 99 percent of your "betting sequences." Generally, the pamphlet writer recommends making a Pass Line bet, or an even-money bet at roulette [the even-money bets are the odd/even; black/red; high/low] and at baccarat of, say, $5 and then doubling it each time it loses until we finally win a bet. The logic is that we have to win a bet sooner or later and, when we do, we get all our losses back plus the initial $5 wager. This is true, as far as it goes, except that the house does not allow wagers to exceed a certain amount. This usually stops a Martingale player somewhere around the eighth or ninth step as the table maximums are $1,000 or $2,000 when the table minimum is $5.

Since the above bets only have a slight edge for the house, they are all more or less very close to a 50-50 proposition. So we'll pretend that they are 50-50 propositions for the purposes of simplicity.

Your first bet is $5. Now, here are the probabilities and the odds of a run of losses.

| Losses in a Row | Wager | Probability | Odds |
|---|---|---|---|
| 1 | $5 | 1 out of 2 | 1 to 1 |
| 2 | $10 | 1 out of 4 | 3 to 1 |
| 3 | $20 | 1 out of 8 | 7 to 1 |
| 4 | $40 | 1 out of 16 | 15 to 1 |
| 5 | $80 | 1 out of 32 | 31 to 1 |
| 6 | $160 | 1 out of 64 | 63 to 1 |
| 7 | $320 | 1 out of 128 | 127 to 1 |
| 8 | $640 | 1 out of 256 | 255 to 1 |
| 9 | $1,280 | 1 out of 512 | 511 to 1 |

The above shows why the pamphlet writer can claim that I will win 99 percent of my "betting sequences" as an eight-step Martingale will be achieved—on average and if *achieved* is the right word—only once every 256 decisions. Still, at 60 decisions an hour at craps, roulette and baccarat (at mini-baccarat we could be facing 150 decisions in an hour) I can expect to hit the wall once every four or five hours. That's an average. It is possible that I could walk up to a table and go to an eight-step the very first time or, conversely, I could play for days without hitting eight losses in a row. The problem is that sooner or later I will hit my share of those eight-step losses and I will wind up losing all my wins back and then some.

The system seller that guarantees his system knows two very important things. Most customers won't ask for their money back. And if they do, he won't give it back. And no system can be guaranteed, or foolproofed. The system I am advocating in this book—a combination of Rhythmic Rolling, *5-Counting*, and Golden Ruling—is what I *believe* to be an advantage-play method. That is, I honestly believe you will have a long-term edge over craps playing this way. But I can't *guarantee* you'll win with it. I can't guarantee *I'll* win with it.

*What was the longest craps roll in history? What was your longest roll? What was the longest roll you ever personally witnessed?*

As there is no official gambling record book, no one knows for sure what the longest roll in history was. However, the longest I ever heard about was by Stanley Fujitake of Hawaii, also known as the Golden Arm, who rolled for approximately 3 hours 45 minutes and made close to 50 passes. This took place at the California Club in Las Vegas. I also heard of someone rolling for three hours at Caesars in Las Vegas. In Tunica, I've heard reports that a man rolled for four hours at Binions but when I made inquiries I found that his roll was actually two hours. In Atlantic City, there are several players who are reputed to have rolled for close two hours plus some. The longest roll I ever witnessed was actually two back-to-back rolls at the Frontier in Las Vegas; both were well over an hour long. Red chip players were playing black and purple chips by the time these two rolls were finished. (Unfortunately, I only saw the rolls, as I was playing blackjack at the time.) The "Arm" in Atlantic City has had many rolls lasting 30 minutes to one hour—often on the same weekend! I have seen a few of these. My longest roll (thus far) is the one I had at Binions on April 2, 1999 when I rolled for a minimum of 45 minutes. I intend to break that record as often as I can!

*What was the worst night you ever had at a craps table?*

I've had many "worst" nights. They are all the same, really. Shooter after shooter actually makes it through the 5-*Count* and then, when I have my money at risk, sevens out on the 6 or 7 or 8 count! I switch tables and the same thing happens. I switch casinos . . . and it continues. I begin to think of the money I've just lost and, even though this money is strictly slated for gambling purposes, what it could have bought in the real world: how many shows I could have seen, how many books I could have read, how many gourmet meals I could have eaten. These negative thoughts always accompany a hammering. Perhaps, the most memorable of my awful nights was at Trump Castle in Atlantic City (now Trump Marina) where both the Captain and I got hammered for two hours.

*Dear Frank:*
*I have had two observations/questions concerning playing the* 5-Count
*and the Doey-Don't on the crap table as described in your book* Beat the
Craps Out of the Casinos.

*First, when using the 5-Count Doey-Don't, I like to use three numbers. Once the 5-Count is complete and I have my three numbers established with odds on the Do side, and the shooter makes his point (which I don't normally have working) I like to lay the odds on the Don't for the Come Out roll only. I feel that this is a real power play as the roller can only pick off one of my points, but if a 7 is rolled I win all three odds bets on the Don't. The odds on the Do are returned since they don't work on the Come Out roll. Once a new point is established the odds on the Don't are taken back and I play the odds on the Do. Everything else I play as described in your book. Your comments please.*

*Second, I have been backed off of the craps table at the Horseshoe in Bossier City, Louisiana for playing the Doey-Don't. The pit boss said that I had to either play the Do or the Don't or bet more on one or the other as the "house doesn't get enough advantage." I took my business elsewhere. In my own mind I have developed a system not exactly described in your book and would like your opinion on its ability to win. I wait the five counts and on the sixth roll I place the 6 and 8 along with a Come bet. I then play as you describe by giving the roller four rolls to hit one of my number and if he doesn't, I them call off my place and odds bets for two rolls and if he still hasn't sevened out call them back on for four rolls. I find that this gets me past the "killer" five or less short rollers and a shot at catching a hot roll. Your comments please.*

*Thank you in advance for taking the time to address these concepts as described. Have a good new year.*

*Pat H.*

*Louisiana*

It seems to me that you are really on top of your game. The variation you use on the Come Out sounds very interesting and I might even give it a try myself. After all, you do have the 7 working for you on the Come Out and those numbers are already up there. If there is such a thing as psychokinesis, the ability to move matter with the mind, you have just about every "mind" rooting for a 7 or 11 on the Come Out. Even if you're dealing with a hot shooter, you return to the "do" after the Come Out and watch him roll. Nice idea.

The problem you encountered at the Horseshoe in Bossier City, Louisiana, has been encountered from time to time by other players using the Captain's methods. Technically, the pit boss was wrong in his assertion that the casino doesn't have enough of an edge because the 12 will appear enough times to give the casino a better edge on the Doey-Don't than it actually has on the Pass or Come—we'll lose 14 times using the doey/don't in 495 decisions while the traditional Pass/Come bettor will lose 7 times in the same number of decisions. So *technically* you're getting the worst of it!

So why does the Captain say use the Doey-Don't as a part of his Supersystem when we're seemingly giving the casino slightly more the best of it? Because the hot shooters the *5-Count* finds are—hopefully—*not* rolling those 7s on the Pass and Come and are instead rolling numbers, glorious numbers! That being the case, we're looking to get those odds payoffs at more-than-even money on all the numbers being hit. The bottom line for the Captain, and for those of us who buy into the Captain's philosophies of play, is this—in the real world, craps isn't always what the math indicates, especially not when shooters roll dem bones! And until craps becomes automated, and the dice are shot out of a little canon, and shooters can no longer touch them, there's more to craps than meets the math.

*What is the Oddsman's bet?*

Not all players who bet the Pass Line want or can afford to take full odds. This is especially true of the games where you have 10X, 20X, and 100X odds. In such cases, with the player's permission, you can place some or all of the odds behind that player's Pass Line number. Just make sure the player is fully aware of the arrangement and doesn't decide at the last second that he deserves the odds win.

The following is a series of letters between me and Kurt Bush that craps players should find interesting as it is indicative of many hundreds of correspondences I've had over the years with players using the *5-Count* and the Captain's methods of play:

*Dear Frank,*
*I used the* 5-Count *on three trips to AC and one trip to Canada. On the three trips to AC, I used the High Roller System to gain a profit of $2,300 and all trips paid. In Canada I used the Doey-Don't and gave back $700. I'm going to Vegas and would like to increase my bets using the High Roller System. Should I just play 6 and 8 for $90 each, or 6 and 8 for $90*

*each and 4/10 for $50, instead of $60 on the 6 and the 8 and $35 on the 4/10?* I would like to say that Beat the Craps Out of the Casinos *is the best book* I've read on craps.

*Thank you,*
*Kurt Bush*

Dear Kurt:

I'm happy you're happy. Here's my advice. In Vegas you will find many casinos that will not charge commission on the 4 or 10 unless you win them! That reduces the house edge by two-thirds. You're facing somewhere around a 1.28 percent edge—better even than the edge for the 6 or 8! So go with three numbers: $60 on the 6 and 8 and $50 on the 4 or 10. If you get hot, go up on both the 4 and the 10. But always use that *5-Count*. Play at the casinos with the commission on winning bets only and at your level of play you should get everything comped and have a damn good shot at winning some more money.

All the best in and out of the casinos.

*Dear Frank,*

*What a week! Six days at The Mirage in Las Vegas, 27.5 hours at the craps table and over $5,000 in profits. Only one losing day, on which I lost $1,400. The 5-Count worked perfectly and playing the 6 and 8 for $60 each and $50 on the 4/10. My wife and I stayed in one of the penthouse suites. On Saturday night, when I went to the host to check on my comps, I was told they would take care of everything, and also would provide a limo to the airport.*

*This was my most extensive use of the 5-Count.*

*A few questions: On two different shoots, the shooter picked up his chips and walked away after hitting his number. The first time this happened, I had three wins and just restarted the 5-Count because it was a new shooter. The second time, I had just pressed my bets and again restarted the 5-Count. Both times I called off my bets. Was this the right move?*

*More than a few times I watched the 5 and 9 get hit time and time*
*again. Is there a way to incorporate them into the High Roller System?*
*Once again, thank you for everything.*
*Kurt Bush*
*P.S. I'm going to Canada next week!*

Dear Kurt:
New shooter, new *5-Count*. Sometimes it's hard to do because
you've been waiting to get into the action and now you have to back
out when a guy walks away from a roll. But make this a law: New
shooter = new *5-Count*.

The 5 and 9 are problematical. They have high edges when
placed (four percent). You could try to buy one or both for $38 and
see if they'll take a $1 commission for it. Or, at Mirage and places that
take commissions on wins only, you could just buy the 5 and 9 (if
they'll allow it) for $50. That would reduce the edge to around 2.5
percent, not great but not as bad as 4 percent. Or, you could get up on
your other numbers and if you see the 5 or 9 showing put up a Come
and go up that way. If they are showing like crazy, and you're ahead,
you might bite the bullet and place them and hope the four percent
doesn't hurt you in the short run.


*Dear Frank,*
*I did not have a good trip in Canada. In all your craps play have you*
*ever seen the dice so cold that it took 33 shooters before a point number got*
*hit? I lost only $1,200 thanks to the* 5-Count.
*Kurt*

Dear Kurt:
Oh yes. This is exactly what the *5-Count* prevents, total devasta-
tion. You still have a profit from your two trips, whereas had you not
played the *5-Count*, you'd be down a lot. Some tables and some days,
it just doesn't happen.

# TWELVE

# The Captain of Craps: His Story

W hen my book *Beat the Craps Out of the Casinos: How to Play Craps and Win!* came out in 1991, it shot to the top of the gaming bestsellers' list where it has remained ever since. The reason? The book introduced to the world of gaming a most remarkable man with the most remarkable ways of analyzing, theorizing and playing craps. That man is the Captain. The book also introduced the world to his fun-loving band of Runyonesque playmates known as the Crew. Since that time, rarely a day goes by when I don't get letters, e-mails, faxes, or phone calls inquiring about, lauding, denying the existence of, disputing or extolling the ideas of, or wanting to meet the Captain. I have received hundreds of requests to introduce individuals to the Captain so that they may become a part of his celebrated Crew.

One man showed up at one of my lectures once and, in the middle of my talk stood up and said: "I demand to see the Captain! I will not stop interrupting your talk until you show me the Captain." He was escorted to see the Captain . . . of the local police.

Letter writers have taken me to task as well. Some nicely. They explain to me that I am hopelessly stupid believing that the *5-Count* can work to offset the house advantage by eliminating poor shooters. Some of the letter writers aren't so nice. Here's one colorful example of someone who wasn't so nice who put me in my place.

Dear Frank Scolete, if that's you're real name, which I doubt
Let me say that you are dumb and a hockster. You must think that all craps player are stupid fools who will fall for anything guy's like you try to sell. There is no "Captain" you just made him up so people wouldn;t think that the dumb ideas in "Beating the Craps from the Casinoes" were your's. Becuase of guy's like you, gambling has a bad name. Becuase of guy's like you, the casinoes make allot of money. They probably pay you to write this crap about craps so they can win all our money. You don't fool me and you don't fool anyone erlse. You are a fraud and you now nothing. People should burn all your books and keep warm in the winter. If the Captain does exit, tell him to jump in the water and drone.
    Your worse nightmere,
    A guy smarter then you!

Another letter writer accused me of "making up the Captain to sell books." Once at the Taj Mahal, an obnoxious, and evidently drunk, player recognized me. "Hey, you're the guy who writes about the admiral. What a joke! There is no admiral!" he informed me. He was right, of course—there is no admiral, but playing right next to him that day was the Captain himself!

Although controversy continues to surround the Captain, his Crew, and his now famous methods of play including the *5-Count*, the *Supersystem*, and his *rhythmic rolling* principle, this controversy seems to have fueled the desire of most people to know more about the Captain as a person and a player.

So, prepare to meet the Captain of craps in a way that no one has ever met him before.

# The Early Years

The Captain's life, a life that started in 1923 in Brooklyn as the son of a fruit store owner and his common-law wife, has been characterized by high drama, O. Henry–like irony, blessed and damnable luck, and over and above all these, a decency of spirit and strength of character that has made him a beloved individual to all who know him, both family and friends, and something of a sucker to unscrupulous individuals and those of low moral character.

"My earliest memory is of my father working. He worked seven days a week in his fruit store. He would get up in the dark of night to go to the New York Fruit Market and get the best fruits and vegetables for his stores."

Before the Great Depression, the Captain's father had five fruit stores in Brooklyn; after it, he had one.

"My father's only diversions from work were betting the horses and making Christmas creches from leftover Christmas trees he couldn't sell at Christmas time. These creches he sold the following Christmas. There was a time when hundreds of his creches were in store windows and churches throughout Brooklyn. He died at the age of 88 after falling down a flight of stairs—carrying a Christmas tree! My mother and father had a rather peculiar marriage, the only thing they shared in common was their love of the horses."

In fact, the Captain's mother's died in Saratoga at the races, "chasing a longshot." She was a true Damon Runyon character in her own right. "She used to take the bus to Aqueduct Raceway just about every day there were races. She enjoyed her beer and scotch. She never went to the doctor and she always called my father Mr. [Last Name], not by his given name. While most of my family were immigrants from Italy and Germany, she was a Irish blueblood who could trace her roots back past the Civil War. She was related to [famous American family] but I think she came from the black sheep side."

While the Captain's mother was in her 80s, she suffered a mild heart seizure at the races and had to be rushed to a hospital in Brooklyn.

"She was in the intensive care unit, in an oxygen tent, and she wasn't happy at all. 'I don't want to die in the hospital,' she kept saying. The doctor was amazed that she was alive at all. He discovered she had diabetes and a whole lot of other stuff wrong with her. He was astonished that she had never been under a doctor's care and had never been really sick, much less hospitalized."

She was also extremely vexed that she would not be allowed to have her scotch or any beer with meals. "On the third or fourth night of her stay, my brother sneaked into her room with a case of beer and put it under the bed in a way that she could reach it. I think he propped up the case on a box. Well, my mother had a grand old time of it that night and the next day, she told the doctor she was ready to leave because she felt much better. The nurses and the doctors and the administration were furious that someone would bring beer to a patient. The following night, my mother left the hospital in her hospital gown and robe, went to a pay phone, called me and said: 'If I am going to die, I want to die in Saratoga.' It was the season, August, and I picked her up, gave her her clothes and we headed for Saratoga. She got to see some races, she lost on each one of them, then she felt her heart giving out. She wanted to stay to see the last race but I insisted we go to the hospital. We got a wheelchair from security and we left. We were going through the bar area when the last race was being run and my mother got to see it in passing. Her horse lost again.

"In the hospital, in the emergency room, I was holding her in my arms, when I felt a small convulsion. She was dying. She looked at me and said: 'You know what I could use right now? A wee bit of scotch.' And she passed on."

The Captain had an older brother and three younger sisters. His brother died in 1985 from complications of diabetes. "My brother was the genius of the family. He was an actor, a master at chess, a boxer and a scholar. But he dropped out of life just when he was about to hit it big as an actor. He had appeared on television several times in the early 50s, had appeared on Broadway, had boxed in the Golden Gloves in New York, had won several championships in chess and he was on his way to having a truly successful life when he just dropped out. He became a carpenter and plumber and spent his days playing chess with another chess master."

The Captain took a different path. While his older brother spent much of his time in solitary pursuits, the Captain was an organizer and a go-getter. "At the age of nine or ten, I was delivering the *New York Mirror* and *The Daily News* to the bars on Fourth Avenue in Brooklyn. My best friend Jimmy and I would buy the papers on DeKalb Avenue in downtown Brooklyn and then we would walk up Fourth Avenue and hit every bar—there was at least a bar on every block or so—and sell the night-owl edition to the men in the bars. In this way I made money for me and my family. This was at the height of the Great Depression."

A popular and athletic teenager, in high school he discovered that he had mathematical and engineering talent, and he was contemplating going to college when World War II broke out. Instead, he enlisted in the army air corps.

"It was not an act of bravery. I enlisted because I didn't want to be drafted into the infantry. I thought the air force would be a better way to go. I was always fascinated by planes and this would give me a chance to learn about them."

The Captain was anything but a natural-born military man. According to his wife: "When the Captain came home on his first leave after boot camp, he looked like the character Sad Sack. His uniform didn't fit, it was all baggy. The shoulders of his jacket drooped. He wasn't an impressive figure at all and some of my girlfriends wondered what I saw in him. This caused my brother, a career military man, the spit-and-shine type, to ride him unmercifully. But the Captain had a good sense of humor and he took it in stride."

In the air corps, the Captain became a turret gunner on the B-17s and B-29s and eventually became a crew chief. "I took my basic training in Atlantic City. I stayed at the Claridge. When the war was over, my wife and I went back to the Claridge for our honeymoon and, for awhile, in the late 1980s and early 1990s, the Claridge was the hotel where the Crew and I spent most of our time in Atlantic City."

After basic training, his first assignment was to Kingman, Arizona where he went to aerial gunnery school. "I was the worst turret gunner in the world. When we would go on training missions we had to shoot at a target and use up all our ammunition. During the final test, I had so much ammunition left that I dumped it out of the plane. The sergeant in charge of the test didn't seem to know or didn't *want* to know what a lousy shot I was—I got a passing score and made it. Truthfully, I don't think I ever hit the target once."

His training continued in Amarillo, Texas, where he went to airplane mechanics school. He became a flight engineer. His skill in servicing aircraft would later serve him well in the post war era when several businesses he owned collapsed. From Texas, he was assigned to a flight crew in Salt Lake City, Utah. That ill-fated crew took its training in Sioux City, Iowa. "I honestly believe that I survived World War II because of luck."

That is an understatement.

"My first crew was about to go to Europe. The day before we were shipping out, I came down with the worst sore throat. I went to the infirmary and found out that I had to have my tonsils removed immediately. I would not be going to Europe with my crew. I objected but I was in no condition to fight—I had a high fever and I was in a lot of pain. So my tonsils were removed. I was in the hospital bed recovering when a doctor came in and informed me that on their very first mission in Europe my crew's plane had been shot down with the loss of everyone on board. I had escaped."

And the Captain's good luck continued: "Instead of going to Europe when I recovered, I was sent to Clark Field in the Philippines. Flying in the Pacific was nowhere near as dangerous as flying over Europe. Also, my best friend from childhood, Jimmy, had been sent to Clark Field. That was a stroke of good fortune."

He and Jimmy must have had their rabbit's feet well-oiled. The first month at Clark Field, the Captain and Jimmy were lounging in the barracks. That evening's entertainment was a movie that the Captain and Jimmy had already seen. "We had seen the movie about five times. It was with Betty Grable and Alice Faye—I forget the name of it now. At first we decided to stay in the barracks and just relax for the night. Then on the spur of the moment I said to Jimmy, 'I don't feel like lounging around. Let's go to the movie even though we've seen it.' As we left the barracks, at that very moment, the Japs launched an attack. Our barracks were demolished and the few people who had decided not to go to the movie were killed."

The Captain and Jimmy had delivered papers together as kids in peacetime to make money and now they pooled their talents to cash in on the war. Neither one smoked, so at first they sold their ration of cigarettes to the other airmen that Uncle Sam, in his benevolent ignorance, was hooking on nicotine. Since neither drank, they were able to make a decent profit from their liquor allotment as well. And what did they do with these profits?

"We ran the craps games!" stated the Captain.

The casino game of craps and the game of craps that was played by the World War II fighting men are two radically different games.

"First of all," said the Captain, "there was no real bank as there is in the casino. Individual players banked the bets as they saw fit. Jimmy and I happened to have a little more money than most of the other guys because we didn't drink or smoke. We didn't drink or smoke not because of any religious thing or anything, we just didn't like to. So, I would book the guys' bets. The game was played on an army blanket against the wall of the barracks. You had to hit the wall. The payoffs were even money for the 6 and 8 which gave anyone who booked the 6 or 8 a nine percent edge because you really should pay off the 6 or 8 at six to five."

Most of the guys who played craps in the service had no idea of the math of the game and the math of the game was heavily in favor of anyone who booked the bets for other than the true odds, which Jimmy and the Captain did. "We ran the games and we made a nice piece of change every payday. After awhile, we gave away the booze and cigarettes—just as the casinos do today—to anyone who played in our game. We had comped players!"

## Shot Down in War and in Life

Although the Captain has stated often that he survived World War II by luck and had a great time doing it, all was not always fun and games for the Captain or for Jimmy. "Jimmy was a ground mechanic. He only had to worry about direct attacks on the base which were few and far between. I had to fly. I hated to fly because we lost planes on takeoff in those days as often as we lost planes in battle—or, at least, it seemed that way. I wish I could say that I was the greatest turret gunner but my rotten record in training was carried over in real warfare. I don't think I ever hit an enemy plane. I'm glad, in a way, because I guess I'm not really responsible for killing another human being, even the enemy."

Although the Captain might not have hit another plane, on his 12th mission, the Captain's plane took a direct hit. "We had to parachute out. We were over an area that while not in enemy possession was not really in our possession either—a kind of no-man's land—or rather a no-man's jungle. It was night. As I was coming down I could hear the Japs shooting at the guys who were lucky to make it out of the plane. I later found out that not one of them survived their landing. They were either killed as they descended or they were captured and killed on the ground. The Japs didn't take prisoners. I landed in a tree with the bombardier, who was seriously injured. We managed to get out of the tree and reach the ground. The bombardier was too hurt to walk so I carried him to a small bridge which [spanned] a small, muddy stream, maybe a half mile or so from where we had landed. We hid under the bridge. The next day, the Jap patrols were everywhere. They had guys who had learned perfect English and these guys would shout out as if they were U.S. servicemen looking to locate us to rescue us. At first it was easy to avoid them because you could tell they weren't American G.I.'s but the enemy. Certain words were pronounced too perfect. Most Americans have an accent of some kind that tells you where they're from. These Jap guys just spoke English too damn good. 'I say, old chap, I'm jolly well from Brooklyn too!'"

But then it became harder for the Captain to tell the real from the unreal because he had caught a frightening case of malaria.

In the subsequent ten days of raging fevers and hallucinations, the Captain and his bombardier—unbeknownst to the Captain now stone dead and decaying—hid under the bridge. "I wasn't eating, I was trying to drink mud, I was almost buried in the mud to cover me, and I wasn't in my right mind. I was having conversations with a man who was beginning to decompose. I had no idea he was dead. I saw him as I *thought* he was—alive and injured. Finally, I made up my mind—what mind I had—that the next patrol, I'd just go up and either let them kill me or they'd be American and I would be saved. I knew that I would die if I just stayed under that bridge. The next patrol, the guy calling out sounded like he came from New York—he said 'terlit' for toilet, and I figured, no Jap would have learned 'terlit' in school. So I called out. I couldn't even walk. I tried to get up but my legs didn't work and I was shivering, so I called out that we were under the bridge. They evidently heard me. I was rescued. The last thing I remember was telling my dead companion that now we would be going home."

The Captain went from a solidly muscled 165 pounds to 132 pounds of skin stretched over bone. It took him many months to recover from the initial malaria and for many weeks it was touch and go whether he would live or die. "I suffered relapses of malaria well into my thirties. They came on unexpectedly. I would shiver violently. I used to scare my own children when that happened."

The malaria was not enough to send the Captain home and, after his recovery, he went back on active duty, this time at Tinian. Then a day he will never forget occurred, a day that was a turning point in the history of mankind.

"This B-29 landed on the runway at Tinian and taxied to the far end of the runway. No one on the base was allowed to go near it. We knew something big was up. But we didn't know what. The crew of that B-29 was not allowed to mix with the other airmen. They went to the officers mess hall and even there they were segregated from the rest of crews. They tried not to look at any of us but we were staring at them. Something was in the air. We all knew that these men were different from the rest of us. These men were on a big mission."

That mysterious B-29 was in fact the Enola Gay, the aircraft that was carrying the first atomic bomb, and it was that moment in history that the Greek gods would have truly feared, the moment when puny man who had once huddled in his caves by the fire that Prometheus had stolen for him, would now rip the guts from the very stuff of existence and make the heavens themselves tremble.

"When I looked at those men, I knew they carried a heavy burden. I didn't exactly know what it was but they were not like the other airmen. Most airmen joked and laughed and used that devil-may-care attitude to cover over any fears they had, these men . . . they were serious, so serious. Now I know why. They had the weight of the world on their shoulders."

After Japan surrendered, the Captain became a part of the force that occupied Japan. "I could have gone home right away but Jimmy and I decided that we wanted to meet the people we had been fighting all these years. Not for revenge. I guess you could say, I wanted to see if they were like us. What is funny, really, strange, is that in Japan I gained a tremendous respect for them and their culture. I realize that they were different, that they had committed many atrocities in the war, but as a people, as individuals, I found that I respected them. I actually made several Japanese friends during the occupation who remained friends for the rest of their lives. They're gone now. Most of the people I knew are gone now."

## Homecoming

The Captain came home from the war in 1946 and the next year he married his high school sweetheart. Both the Captain and his mate decided to keep their family small. "I never wanted my children to experience any hardships. I knew that the more kids you had, the harder it is to give them all the things you want to give. I wanted to give them a lot." The Captain had a son and a daughter.

Both of the Captain's children have nothing but praise for their father. The son said: "He's the best father a boy could ever have and he's my best friend now that I'm a man." The daughter stated: "He's always there when you need him. He is always full of love."

In the postwar era, the Captain made a decision that would characterize his life. "I decided to go into business for myself rather than work for someone else. Television had just come out so I opened a small television store in Brooklyn—sales and service. Again to be perfectly honest, I was not a good businessman. Most television sets were beyond the reach of most people at the time, so I would tell people they could buy on time and pay me when they could. A lot of people took advantage of that and a lot of people took advantage of me and never paid up. I remember one fellow in particular, a Swedish guy, Johansen, who used to stop by the store and watch the sets in the window—I had the sets on all day. Every night he'd come out of the subway, which was just a few yards from my store and he'd stop and look at the sets. Finally, I couldn't bear it anymore and I went out to him. In broken English, he introduced himself and I told him that he could take whichever set he wanted and pay me back when he could. He was so happy. Over time he paid me back, I guess. I never really kept track." Although the Captain thought that the generous offering of the television was the end of the Johansen story, it was really only the beginning as future events would bear out.

Still business boomed for the Captain because in those days America was going television crazy and everyone wanted sets, and then everyone eventually needed those sets serviced. The Captain supplied both needs.

"My business was doing quite nicely and I was able to provide for my family. But then I made a big mistake."

The Captain started to bet heavily on the horses. Without his wife's knowledge, the Captain was playing 50-50 with the family funds. On everything that he made, he gave half to his family and business but he took the other half to play the ponies. This routine lasted for more than 15 years.

"I estimate that I lost a total of one and a half million dollars at the track or to bookies in my lifetime. I was making good money in my business and no one knew that I was spending a fortune on the horses. Oh, I had some spectacular wins, and some people were under the impression that I was a great horse handicapper. I was not. I was a great horse player and a great loser. It took me 15 years to realize that I was not a great horse handicapper—not good enough to turn a profit anyway—and I wasn't going to overcome the 17 or so percent edge that the track has on a player."

But horses never bankrupted the Captain. People did. In business, he made good money. But he spent good money too. He was a soft touch for friends and family. Anyone who needed money knew they could come to the Captain and borrow—and he never pestered them to pay it back and he never charged interest. "Many people just took the money and I'd never hear from them or I would never mention it to them when I did see them. I always felt that you were honor-bound to pay back a loan. Not everyone felt the same way."

Then a series of devastating business decisions cost the Captain his livelihood. "In the early 1960s, the competition for television repairs and service became very intense in New York, particularly with the advent of affordable color televisions. Instead of being the only store in the neighborhood, I was now competing with dozens of other stores who had big businesses backing them. I was an independent operator. The department stores were also in the business and their prices were hard to match. So I decided to go into the discount business in addition to television. A friend got me interested and I put every penny I had into several stores in Manhattan which this friend was to oversee while I handled my store in Brooklyn."

The Captain didn't know it but his "friend" was robbing him blind to pay off gambling debts he owed to rather unsavory characters. Unlike the Captain, who was doing his 50 percent for his family, 50 percent for his gambling habit routine, the "friend" was doing 110 percent into the gambling habit and to-hell-with-everything-and-everyone-else routine. The friend had asked for, and the Captain had foolishly given him, the power to write checks against the business. The "friend" cooked the books for several years and then finally the Captain found out what was going on. "I found out when some beefy guys showed up at my apartment to tell me that I owed them this incredible sum of money. They were collectors for a loan-shark who had lent money to my business through my friend. My friend had run off several days before. I found out about it when someone called me to ask why my stores were closing. I had no idea they were closing. I was a dope, plain and simple."

Correct that—the Captain was a *broke* dope.

# What Goes Around, Comes Around

If Caesar had his Brutus, so did the Captain. Betrayed by a "friend" with whom he had entered into a chain of Manhattan stores, the Captain now faced a very real threat to his livelihood, if not his life. To keep his reputation (and perhaps to save his life) he negotiated a settlement with the loan-shark to pay off the debts that his business (through his "friend") had incurred.

"I sold the store, and I went to work for the airline industry. I was a good mechanic so I took the test. I passed. I worked the night shift. I paid off the loan-shark over a number of years from the sale of my business and from a percentage of my salary. In the day, I studied to take the real estate exam. I was always good with people and I figured real estate might be a way to recover my life."

For several years the Captain worked at Kennedy Airport at night and tried to learn the ropes of New York's highly competitive real estate industry by day. "I wanted to go into commercial real estate because not only was that where the money was, but I felt it fit my temperament. I found a piece of property in New York City—a nice-sized lot that would make a great site for an office building. With what I had managed to save over the last few years and what I could borrow, I bought the lot. I then put an advertisement in the newspaper describing the lot and I left my name and phone number. This was my first big real estate speculation and everything I had was riding on it. For a week no one answered the ad and I thought that I had gone all in on this investment only to go broke again. I was kicking myself in the behind. Then I got a call. The man had a slight accent and he asked me if I was the same guy who had owned a television store in Brooklyn. I said yes I was. He then said that he was going to buy the lot from me and that he was going to put up a ten-story office building and, when it was finished, I would be in charge for the rest of my life with renting each and every office to tenants— at a substantial commission. I said to him that he hadn't even seen the property yet and he didn't even know me. He said: 'I don't have to see the property because I do know you. You're the man who helped me get my first television set! I have never forgotten you and what a good man you are.' It was Johansen, the man the Captain had given a television to when he first started in business. "Johansen had

become a multimillionaire who owned dozens of buildings throughout the New York area."

That one deal made the Captain a millionaire himself and to this
day the Captain still rents out the office space in the building.
"Johansen died but he left in his will that as long as I live, I am the
only real estate agent to handle this property."

From the moment that the multimillionaire Johansen gave the
Captain his first break in real estate, the Captain soared high in the
highly competitive New York real estate market. He was a natural-
born advantage-player, one who structured deals so that everyone
could win. He bought, sold, and brokered high-powered commercial
real estate throughout the New York metropolitan area. Through the
late 1970s, he had amassed quite a fortune. In addition to commissions, he owned large real estate holdings on Long Island and in
upstate New York, some of them purchased on the highly speculative
assumption that casino gambling would be introduced to the areas
where these properties were.

Still, the Captain remained a soft touch for both friends and rel-
atives. At one point, he was supporting an unemployed relative and
her four kids, and a nephew who had become addicted to gambling
and was in recovery. The Captain paid off $20,000 of this young
man's gambling debts to get the loan-sharks off his back. He also
made generous loans with no interest to several other individuals
who had been hit with hard times and were relying on the Captain to
bail them out. The Captain did. Some of these people paid the
Captain back, or attempted to, but many more just took his money
and ran.

"I guess money never meant that much to me, except as a way
to help people, or have fun. I never pinched pennies and I never wor-
ried about whether I would get back my money when I gave it to
friends. I am a Depression-era guy. I saw enough suffering. If my
money could alleviate some of it for some people, then I helped."

# Atlantic City

With the arrival of gambling in Atlantic City, a whole new era
opened for the East Coast and for the Captain. "I had given up the
horses and was getting my gambling high from real estate. But many
of my friends kept insisting that Atlantic City was the place to go. I

had made several trips to Vegas in the 1970s but I was not a big play-er. I just paid for everything and enjoyed myself. I played craps the traditional way—I made a Pass Line bet and backed it with odds and maybe I'd place the 6 and 8. I knew the math was against me so I never took the game that seriously."

But his friends insisted that he join them on a trip to Atlantic City in 1978. "We went to Resorts. The place was packed. I played the same way that I had when I was in Las Vegas. I could see that craps was a losing proposition from the get-go, so I didn't invest much time or energy in it."

For those with sporting blood in the New York area, the rise of Atlantic City created a whole new culture—the weekend high roller (or "weekend warriors" as many casino executives call them). People who had formally made maybe one or two trips a year (if that many) to Las Vegas were going down to Atlantic City in droves on a regular basis, mostly weekends, some on every weekend. Unfortunately, as they were going down to the shore, their bank accounts were going down the drain. By the late 1980s, Atlantic City's dozen casinos made as much money as all of the casinos in Vegas combined. The reason had to do with the phenomenal number of high rollers from the East Coast who were playing there.

"I realized after going down occasionally that if I wanted to go on weekends, and if I wanted to get everything comped, I was going to have to come up with some way to cut my losses which were steadily mounting. So I watched the game intensely and I watched the pit intensely and, as you wrote in *Beat the Craps Out of the Casinos*, I literally stumbled on the *5-Count* which I used as a way to get a lot of comps with a much reduced risk. As I played the *5-Count*, I slow-ly saw that not only was I getting these comps but I was gradually coming out ahead at the game. It was an evolutionary process of stumbling on the *5-Count*, and then creating methods of play using the *5-Count* as the key variable."

Knowing that the *5-Count* worked, the Captain tried to figure out why it worked. He studied shooters and surmised that perhaps the real game of craps was not really as random as everyone thought. "I began to notice that I saw more good rolls among those shooters who took care with their rolls than with shooters who just flung the dice down the table. In any random game, there will be wild swings, crazy streaks, and some shooters who just flung the dice did have good, even great rolls. But overall and over time, it was very clear to me that shooters who set the dice and gently lofted them to the end of the table without much bouncing tended to have better rolls."

"As I was learning more and more about craps, I was also playing more and more. In the late 1980s, I made some awful real estate deals in upstate New York that really cost me. After that I found I was spending almost as much time in Atlantic City as I was spending time doing real estate deals."

It was during the early and mid 1980s that the Captain began the process of collecting his Crew. It was not a conscious effort. "I never had the intention of surrounding myself with a bunch of Damon Runyon–type characters; it just happened." It happened for a reason. The Captain has the kind of personality that attracts people. He is Runyonesque himself.

Most of the Crew were business acquaintances or "friends from the neighborhood" who had money and enjoyed going down to Atlantic City as a group. Some were friends that the Captain had had for years. Russ, the breather, had gone to elementary school with the Captain. They were reunited at a craps table.

"I was playing and I suddenly heard this gravelly voice yelling out 'Hard ten. Hard ten!' Remember Froggy from *Our Gang* comedies [also known as *The Little Rascals*]? Well that was Russ's voice. I looked up and there he was. I called over to him and we were inseparable from that day to the day of his death several years ago from emphysema."

At its height, the Captain's Crew had 22 members, all high rollers. In addition to Russ, the breather; there was Jimmy P., the enthusiastic First Mate, who won so much money in such a short period in the mid 1990s that both he and the Captain became *persona non grata* at the Tropicana (then Tropworld), a property that had the temerity to circulate a memo advising other casinos that these two men should be "watched carefully" when they played. Jimmy P. told me: "I don't quite know what they were supposed to watch for. It's all spelled out in your books. There was no mystery in how the Captain and I were playing."

There was the Doctor, a surgeon and expert card counter in blackjack whose greatest desire was to operate on the casinos' bankrolls. In fact, the Doctor once saved the life of a man at the Claridge who had keeled over with an apparent heart attack when this man had parlayed three hard sixes in row!

There was the "Arm," a legend in her own right, a woman who, by all reports and by my own eyes' witness, seemed to have an uncanny control of the dice. I have seen the crowds at a craps table part like the Red Sea before Moses when the "Arm" approached to roll them bones. Once at a table, other players (all Crew members) passed up their turns to roll so that the dice would return to the "Arm" time and time again. Although not every roll she had that night was epic, there were enough good and excellent rolls for the Captain and Crew to hit the casino to the tune of six figures in a little under three hours. The next night, the members of the Crew were about to do the same thing—pass up their rolls to let the "Arm" roll exclusively—when suddenly a new rule was invoked by the casino pit boss—*the same person can't roll the dice time and time again*. I only heard of that rule that night in that particular casino and I've never heard of it again.

Then there was John the Analyzer, who saw patterns in everything and omens in all. He was an extremely superstitious man who would do a host of rituals before he played and, especially, when it was his turn to roll the dice. Like Ed Norton [Art Carney] of *Honeymooners* fame, the "Analyzer" could infuriate a pit crew by his deliberations and concatenations before he rolled. For example, when it was his turn to shoot, he would take all five dice and throw them against the wall nearest him. The dice that came up with the same sides, he would then roll again (if there were three or more) until just two dice showed doubles. Then he would set these dice one atop the other with the six-spots at the bottom and the one-spot at the top. Then he twisted the die on top so that the sides of the two dice showed seven all around. His belief was incorporated into this chant, which he said just before he rolled: "Seven on the side, devil takes a ride!" (The "devil" is a term used by superstitious players so they don't have to say the word "seven.")

There was Vic, the man who learned basic strategy in blackjack in one afternoon. Vic was one of the most generous guys you'd ever want to meet. One day a beggar outside the Taj Mahal in Atlantic City asked Vic for a quarter for "something to eat." Vic gave him a green chip [worth $25)! A half hour later at the craps table, Vic noticed the beggar playing and said to him: "I thought you wanted that quarter for a meal?" and the beggar replied: "I decided to try for a gourmet one."

There was the hot-tempered Joe, who was not adverse to having his voice rise several octaves above the din of the casino when he didn't get what he wanted. There was also Fearful Frank T., who often called off his bets as the dice were in midair, so fearful was he of losing. There was Connie, and Helen, and Phil the Forgetful. And Sal, and Jo the Wanderer, and the youngest members of the group, Annette and Dave, and finally there was me and the beautiful A.P. In the intervening years since the writing of my first book on the Captain in 1991, some of the Crew have died: Vic, Frank T., Russ the Breather, and Jimmy P. Several more have moved to Florida.

Throughout the mid and latter part of the 1980s and well into the 1990s, however, the Captain and his Crew of high rollers became legendary in Atlantic City—especially among the casino hosts and player-development executives who vied with one another to book them into their hotels. A few knew that while many of the Crew were losing bundles of cash, the Crew members who played the Captain's way were actually taking home money and/or getting a truckload of comps without a truckload of risk.

In the excellent book *How to Be Treated Like a High Roller Even Though You're Not One* (Carol Publishing) former Claridge President Robert Renneisen has a curious passage about a group of high rollers who had been hitting the Claridge for rather large wins and rather large comps during this time period. In fact, I surmise that Renneisen is referring to the Captain and several of his Crew who had been hitting the Claridge hard during that particular time (I know because I was with them) using the *5-Count* to rack up comp points without the attendant risk. Here's Renneisen's description of the events:

"One common mistake [in issuing comps] made by casino hosts is to base all of their decisions on theoretical win, or 'points.'

"We once had a host, I'll call him Mike, who loved to write comps. He had a rather large following of players who knew how to take advantage of the system. They came frequently and would quickly leave when they were unlucky, rarely losing much. When they were winning, however, they would bet enormous sums and rack up a lot of 'points' in the rating system.

"Frankly, they were smart players. . . . Finally one day I asked Mike about all the comps he'd written for players who consistently beat the hell out of us. 'Well, boss,' he said proudly, 'Look at the [comp] points these guys have. . . .'"

"Mike" wound up leaving the Claridge and so did the Captain and his Crew, who found the situation more to their liking at several other Atlantic City properties at the time.

This "Mike" that Renneisen is referring to is now a big executive at another Atlantic City casino and he still comps the Captain and his Crew. Several years ago "Mike" asked me to autograph a copy of *Beat the Craps Out of the Casinos: How to Play Craps and Win!* for his father, who was taking up the game. "If my father is going to play craps, he might as well play the best way. The Captain has hammered us for years."

From 1990 on, the story of the Captain, his ideas, his insights, his methods of play have all been on the public record. In video tapes, audio cassettes, books and articles, I have attempted to do justice to the greatest craps player who ever lived.

# Afterword

# The Limits of
# Anecdotal Evidence

I recognize that the mere fact that I assert that the Captain has been winning for over 20 years at a game where the house has the mathematical edge, makes me somewhat suspect in orthodox gaming circles. I would be skeptical, too, if I hadn't been there, seen it, and verified the facts. I can't and won't deny what I have experienced and what casino executives have told me.

There is no mysticism or secrets to the Captain's methods of play. I write about them straightforwardly in my books and articles, I talk about them honestly and in detail in my audio cassettes. I can't guarantee that if you play as the Captain plays you will win. I wish I could.

At the heart and soul of the Captain's philosophy is, of course, the *5-Count*, a method for avoiding horrendous shooters and finding good shooters. The underlying assumption of the Captain's philosophy is that a small but real minority of players are rhythmic rollers who might be subtly altering the odds of the game. To find these individuals, you have to have some means of hanging onto your money as you play. I have covered these ideas in the book you have read.

I have even gone further and made it clear that I do firmly believe that by utilizing the Captain's principles and by following the Golden Ruler, it is possible to get a real advantage at craps. I can't prove that contention beyond a shadow of a doubt, because my evidence is merely anecdotal and based on my experience and the testimony of others; but I think I have proven it sufficiently to myself and I hope I have, at the very least, perked your interest in attempting to beat the game of craps by using the *5-Count*, developing your own rhythmic roll, and utilizing the Golden Ruler. Playing this way has no real economic downside. You can speculate that I am wrong about the Captain and his methods; that I'm insane to think people can control the dice and that the Golden Ruler is the way to capitalize on such rhythmic rollers, and you might think that I am seriously misguided in thinking that you can become a rhythmic roller yourself by finding your own method for rolling them bones. You can also speculate that the Captain's nearly quarter century of winning at craps is just some unique fluctuation in randomness, kind of a gambling singularity—like the universe is a physical singularity—that can't be duplicated by any other players.

You can speculate anything you want really. But so what? The Captain has done what the Captain has done, you take it or you leave it, you believe it or don't. Many years ago I was reading a science book that stated the bumblebee shouldn't be able to fly based on what was known of aerodynamics. The problem was that these damn bees did fly. Either you reject the evidence of your own experience:

"Hey, Mommy, what's that?"

"Oh, that's a bumblebee, Timmy."

"But my science teacher says they can't fly and that one is flying!"

"Your science teacher should get out to the park more often and check out the real world. Bumblebees have always flown, son."

Or you go with known aerodynamics:

"Timmy, you got question number seven wrong. Bumblebees can't fly. Next time study your notes and don't be wasting your time at the park so often."

Or you say to yourself:

"There must be something else going on that we haven't figured in our equations because bumblebees fly."

Over time I think the reasons for the bumblebee's flight have been solved. I think the reason for the Captain's success has been solved too. In the real world, craps is a physical game that can be overcome by a physical method. A small percentage of shooters are altering the math of the game by the way they shoot. The Captain "stumbled" onto a method of finding these shooters and he was intelligent enough to recognize it for what it was—a technique that could give him a slight edge.

If you follow the advice in this book, you can only help yourself; you can't hurt yourself. You'll still get into the action, risk far less money in your lifetime of play, get far more comps than you deserve, and still get the thrill of pitting your Davidian bankroll against the Goliaths of gaming. And that should be enough to whet any craps player's appetite for combat.

Time has not dimmed the Captain's enthusiasm for craps, nor his winning ways. He keeps meticulous records of his sessions and his comps. Although he no longer plays several times a week, he does play several times a month. The loss of some of the core Crew members such as Jimmy and Russ has hurt, but the Captain can still bring down to the shore some of the biggest high rollers in the New York area. He just doesn't do it as often. As Frank Sinatra was to the casino stages, so too is the Captain to the gaming stage—a legend whose like we will never see again. He did it his way—and it worked!

# Glossary

*Action*: The amount and type of betting a player does in the casino. The longer a player plays, the bigger the bettor bets, the more action he gives the casino. All ratings of players are based on the total action they give the casino.

*Advantage Play*: The ability of some players to get an edge over the casino. Techniques used to get the edge over the casino.

*Any Craps*: A one roll bet. The next roll of the dice will be 2, 3, or 12. A Crazy Crapper bet and not recommended.

*Any Seven*: A one roll bet. The next roll of the dice will be a 7. A Crazy Crapper bet and not recommended.

*Back Line*: Another term for the Don't Pass Line.

*Bankroll*: The total stake a player has to gamble with.

*Banning*: The practice by Nevada casinos of barring advantage players.

*Barnacles*: Low-limit players, usually $5.00 bettors, who hang out with the Crew.

*Bar the 12*: The 12 does not win for Wrong bettors on the Come Out roll. It is a tie. This gives the casino an edge over the player. Some casinos bar the 2 rather than the 12.

*Big 6 and Big 8*: An even money bet that either the 6 or 8 will come up before the 7. A Crazy Crapper bet and not recommended.

*Boxman*: The seated supervisor at the center of the craps table.

*Buck*: Another term for the black/white disk used to delineate which number is the shooter's point.

*Buy the 4 or the 10*: Giving a 5 percent tax to the casino in order for the 4 and the 10 to be paid off at correct odds of two to one when they are placed. A poor bet unless used exactly as the Captain outlines in the High Roller System, or at those casinos that only charge the commission on a winning bet.

*Center Field*: The number 9 in the Field section on the craps layout.

*Chasing Your Losses*: Increasing your bets when you're losing in order to make back your money. Or, placing Crazy Crapper bets to get bigger payoffs. A poor way to recoup and not recommended.

*Cold Dice* or *Cold Table*: When the dice aren't passing and shooters are sevening out early in their rolls. A losing table.

*Come Bet*: Betting that the dice will repeat a number established after placing a bet in the Come Box. Similar to a Pass Line bet.

*Come Out*: Rolls of the dice before a point has been established. Usually referred to as the Come Out roll.

*Comp*: Free goods and services given to players in exchange for their action. Complimentaries.

*Craps*: The roll of a 2, a 3, or a 12. On the Come Out roll the stickman will call "Craps out!" when these numbers are rolled.

*Crazy Crapper Bets*: Big odds bets where the house takes a heavy tax out of the player's winnings. A Crazy Crapper is a person who makes these bets.

*The Crew*: The name for the group of high rollers which travels with the Captain. Also the term for the four dealers at the craps table.

*Dealer*: Name for any casino personnel who works a game.

*Devil ("The devil jumped up!")*: Another name for the 7. An expression for sevening out.

*Die*: Singular of dice.

*Discretionary Removal*: The ability in Place betting to call off or remove your bets. Odds bets are also discretionary.

*Disk*: Two-sided black and white circular device that designates which point number is the shooter's.

*Doey-Don't*: Betting both the Pass Line/Don't Pass Line and the Come/Don't Come sides of the board.

*Don't Come Bet*: A bet made against the dice representing a number established by placing a bet in the Don't Come Box. Similar to a Don't Pass bet.

*Don't Pass Bet*: A bet make on the Come Out roll that the dice will not repeat the point number established before a seven is rolled.

*Easy Way*: The opposite of a Hard Way, where the numbers 4, 6, 8, and 10 are made with any combination but a pair. 3:1 is an easy 4.

*Edge*: The amount, usually expressed as a percentage, of advantage that the house has over a player.

*Even Money*: A bet paid off at $1.00 for $1.00.

*Fair Game*: A game that theoretically doesn't favor the house or the player. Given a sufficiently long playing time, the game would end up a draw. In craps a fair game would be to pay off all bets at their true odds.

*Field Bet*: A bet that the next roll of the dice will be any of the following numbers: 2, 3, 4, 9, 10, 11, or 12. A Crazy Crapper bet and not recommended.

*5-Count*: The revolutionary system developed by the Captain to avoid horrendous rolls of the dice, stretch the amount of time your money gives you at the table, and position you to take advantage of good rolls.

*Fixing the Dice*: The setting of specific numbers or the arrangement of the dice a specific way by the shooter before he rolls.

*Floorman*: The person who supervises a portion of the pit under the direction of a pit boss.

*Fluctuation in Probability*: Sequences of numbers appearing out of proportion to their probability.

*Free Odds*: A bet made behind the Pass/Don't Pass or the Come/Don't Come wager that is paid off at true odds. Free odds are fair odds.

*Gambling Stake*: The amount of money specifically set aside for gambling purposes only.

*Golden Shooter*: A person who sets the dice a certain way each time and then takes care with his or her rolls.

*Hard Way Bets*: A bet that the numbers 4, 6, 8, or 10 will be made as 2:2, 3:3, 4:4, or 5:5 respectively before a seven is rolled. Crazy

Crapper bets and not recommended unless you are a rhythmic roller who knows without question you can overcome high house edge on these bets.

*Heat*: The psychological pressure that a casino can put on a player. The casino is placing heat on a player when the pit personnel take a more than casual notice of him or constantly question him about his method of play. In blackjack, casino heat has resulted in the banning of card counters and other skilled players from casinos in Nevada. The Supersystem on occasion will draw some casino heat, as will rhythmic rolling.

*Higher and Higher*: The Captain's method for increasing bets during a good roll. Used in the Limited Bankroll System as discussed in *Beat the Craps Out of the Casinos: How to Play Craps and Win*.

*High Roller*: The term for individuals who bet large sums of money.

*High Roller System*: The Captain's method of play for large stakes that reduces the house edge and stretches your time at the table. Involves precise use of *5-Count* and intelligent place betting strategies as discussed in *Beat the Craps Out of the Casinos: How to Play Craps and Win*.

*Hop Bet*: A one roll bet on any number the player wants. A Crazy Crapper bet and not recommended.

*Horn Bet*: A one roll bet that any one of the following numbers will appear on the next roll: 2, 3, 11, 12. A Crazy Crapper bet and not recommended.

*Horrendous Rolls*: Rolls where the shooter sevens out within a few rolls after establishing a point number.

*Hot Dice* or *Hot Table*: Rolls of the dice where numbers and points are being made and the 7 is nowhere to be seen. A winning table.

*House Odds*: Odds paid out to place bets and Crazy Crapper bets that are not true odds, House takes tax out of winnings.

*Inside Numbers*: The place numbers 5, 6, 8, 9.

*Law of Repeating Numbers*: A term for the Captain's belief that numbers tend to repeat.

*Lay Bet*: A place bet against the number being rolled before a 7 appears. Paid off at house odds.

*Lay the Odds*: An odds bet placed by the Wrong bettor that the 7 will appear before the number is rolled.

*Limited Bankroll System*: The name for the Captain's system for players who don't wish to play the Supersystem or find it too demanding. Also, for those players with limited funds. Discussed in *Beat the Craps Out of the Casinos: How to Play Craps and Win*.

*Long Run*: The concept that a player could play so often that probability would tend to even out. That is, you'd start to see the total appearance of numbers approximating what probability theory suggests. A long run player is one who intends to play a lot.

*Money at Risk*: Money that when wagered can be lost. In the Supersystem, odds bets on the Come and the initial Come roll where the 12 loses for the player.

*Money Not-At-Risk*: Money that is on the layout but cannot be lost. Bets that have been called off. Bets that cancel out as in Come/Don't Come.

*Monster Roll*: A hot roll where numbers and points are coming and the 7 is nowhere to be seen. The roll lasts a minimum of a half hour. "The Arm" is known affectionately as "The Queen of the Monsters."

*Nickel Chips*: Term for $5.00 chip. The Captain doesn't recommend thinking of money as chips.

*Non-Seven Mode*: Roll in which a rhythmic roller is positioning and rolling the dice in such a way that the 7 doesn't appear. Can be taken advantage of by an expert player.

*No Second Guess / No-Guess Rule*: A tongue-in-cheek rule that the Captain recommends so you don't castigate yourself for making wrong guesses as discussed in *Beat the Craps Out of the Casinos: How to Play Craps and Win*.

*Numbers*: The numbers 4, 5, 6, 8, 9, 10.

*Off ("Take my bets off.")*: A verbal call that some or all of a player's bets will not be working on this and/or subsequent rolls. Any bet that is not working.

*One-Roll Bets*: Bets determined by the next roll of the dice only.

*On ("My bets are on")*: A verbal call that some or all of the player's bets are working. Any bet that is working.

*Out and Up Progression*: The Captain's method in the Supersystem and the Limited Bankroll System for having more numbers working and then more money on the table as discussed in *Beat the Craps Out of the Casinos: How to Play Craps and Win*.

*Outside Numbers*: The numbers 4, 5, 9, 10.

*Pass*: The point number being made.

*Pass Line*: The area of the layout where a Pass Line bet is made.

*Pass Line Bet*: Bet that the dice will make the shooter's number before a seven appears.

*Payoff, Payout*: The paying of a winning bet by the casino.

*Pilgrim's Progression*: The Captain's method for getting more money on the table during a hot roll. To be used in the High Roller System as discussed in *Beat the Craps Out of the Casinos: How to Play Craps and Win*.

*Pit*: The working area for casino personnel inside a group of tables of the same game.

*Pit Boss*: The supervisor of the entire pit.

*Place Bets*: A bet placed directly on any, some, or all of the numbers: 4, 5, 6, 8, 9, 10.

*Point*: The number the shooter must make before a seven is rolled.

*Point Numbers*: The numbers 4, 5, 6, 8, 9, 10.

*Pressing a Bet ("Press it!")*: To increase a bet, usually by doubling it, after a win.

*Proposition Bets*: Bets in the middle of the layout. These are all Crazy Crapper bets and not recommended.

*Push*: Term for a tie in gambling.

*Pushing the House* or *Pushing the Casino*: The term coined by the Captain to describe a player placing more money in odds behind the Pass or Come bets than is indicated by the casino. Making the casino give you a better game than advertised. The Captain has been credited with the Pushing of Atlantic City. A recommended technique for getting more money on the table at correct odds.

*Qualified Shooter*: A shooter who has already made a point. This concept has been the basis of several systems in craps. An interesting but archaic way to play in light of the Captain's revelations.

*Quarter Chips*: The term for $25.00 chips. The Captain does not recommend thinking of money as chips.

*Rails*: Another term for the grooved area where players keep their chips.

*Rating*: The casino's appraisal of a player's action to determine the level of his comps.

*RFB*: The expression used to indicate that a player is fully comped by the casino. Literally means room, food, and beverage. The Captain and his Crew are all RFB.

*Rhythmic Roller*: The Captain's term for a shooter who rolls the same way over and over in a set rhythm. Such a shooter can get into a non-seven mode and be exploited by an expert player.

*Right Bettor*: A player betting with the dice and against the 7.

*Ruin or Element of Ruin*: Losing every penny of your gambling stake. The possibility of losing every penny of your gambling stake.

*Scared Money*: Money the player is afraid to lose because he cannot afford to. Money not set aside specifically for gambling.

*Session Stake*: The amount of money specifically set aside for a single session at the tables.

*Seven-Out*: The 7 being rolled after a point was established. All Right bets lose on a seven out.

*Shoot*: All the rolls of a single shooter until he sevens-out.

*Shooter*: The player rolling the dice.

*Short Run*: A limited time at the tables where numbers may fluctuate sharply from probability. A short-run player is one who plays infrequently.

*Sitckman*: The dealer calling the game and carrying the big stick.

*Supersystem*: The Captain's ultimate system, the dynamic combination of the *5-Count* and the Doey-Don't.

*Take the Odds*: Free odds bets behind the Pass Line and Come bets that are paid off at correct odds.

*Tapped Out*: Losing your session stake or your entire bankroll.

*Tax*: The amount of money the casino takes out of winning bets. Vigorish or vig.

*Toke*: A tip for the dealers.

*Tough Out*: A player who doesn't beat himself. A player who through skill, insight, and intuition has the potential to hurt the casino's bankroll. Players who effectively put the Captain's methods into play.

*Vigorish, Vig*: A gambler's term for the house edge. Heard less and less in casino circles.

*Virgin Principle*: The superstition that a female who has never rolled the dice before will have a hot roll the first time out.

*Wager*: A bet.

*Working ("My bets are working!")*: A verbal call that bets are on. Bets are on a can be lost.

*Wrong Bettor*: A player who bets against the dice and with the 7.

# Index

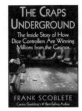

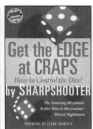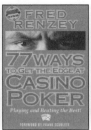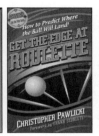